2025 IGE Distinguished Lecture Forum

한국 정치·안보 위기 긴급 진단:
트럼프 2.0 한미동맹의 미래와 대북전략 변화

초판 1쇄 발행 2025년 4월

펴낸이 전광우
지　원 김경진, 김시연
디자인 김정진
인　쇄 한진기획인쇄

펴낸곳 세계경제연구원
전　화 02-551-3334~8
팩　스 02-551-3339
등　록 서울시 강남구 영동대로 511

종이책 ISBN 979-11-6177-050-5 [03320]

종이책 정가 15,000원

*이 책은 저작권법에 따라 보호받는 저작물이므로 무단 전재와 복제를 금합니다.
*잘못된 책은 구입하신 서점에서 바꾸어 드립니다.

2025 IGE Distinguished Lecture Forum

한국 정치·안보 위기 긴급 진단: 트럼프 2.0 한미동맹의 미래와 대북전략 변화

Victor Cha

한국 정치·안보 위기 긴급 진단: 트럼프 2.0 한미동맹의 미래와 대북전략 변화

빅터 차
(Victor Cha)

빅터 차
Victor Cha

　미국 외교정책 및 대외전략 분야의 국제적 권위자로 미 조지타운대학교 석좌교수로 재직 중이며, 미국 국제전략문제연구소(CSIS)의 지정학·외교담당 소장이자 한국석좌를 맡고있다. 그 이전에는 백악관 국가안전보장회의의 아시아 담당 국장과 부시 행정부에서 북한 특별 보좌관을 역임했다.

[2025년 1월 17일]

한국 정치 · 안보 위기 긴급 진단:
트럼프 2.0 한미동맹의 미래와 대북전략 변화

빅터 차
미 조지타운대학교 석좌교수
CSIS (국제전략문제연구소) 지정학 · 외교담당 소장 및 한국석좌

전광우 이사장: IGE 포럼에 오신 여러분을 진심으로 환영합니다. 2025년 IGE 웨비나 시리즈의 첫 웨비나의 특별연사로 미국 외교정책, 특히 동북아시아 관련 세계적인 권위자이신 빅터 차 박사를 모시게 되어 매우 기쁘고 영광으로 생각합니다. 도널드 트럼프 미 대통령의 취임이 다음 주로 다가온 만큼 관련된 글로벌 지정학적 도전과 미중 간의 지속적인 긴장, 북한과 러시아 간 동맹 강화를 비롯한 한국이 직면한 외교 및 안보 관련 주요 현안들에 대해 깊이 있는 논의를 진행할 예정입니다. 특히 한국이 정치적 혼란 가운데 트럼프 2기를 맞이하는 만큼, 한국에 대한 전략적 시사점에 대해 심도 있는 인사이트를 나눌 것으로 기대합니다.

빅터 차 박사님은 현재 미 조지타운대학교의 석좌교수이시며, 2023년에는 조지타운대학교 종신직 교수에게 주어지는 최고 명예인 'Distinguished University Professor'로 임명되신 바 있습니다. 미 국제전략문제연구소(CSIS)의 지정학 · 외교담당 소장

및 한국석좌도 맡고 계십니다. 또한, 백악관 국가안전보장회의 아시아 담당 국장을 역임하셨으며, 조지 W 부시 대통령 행정부에서는 대북 정책 수석 고문을 지내시기도 했습니다.

그 어느 때 보다 혼돈의 시기인 만큼 차 박사님께서도 연초부터 출장이 많으신데, 오늘은 하와이에서 접속하고 계십니다. 그럼 이제 소개를 마치고 차 박사님을 모시겠습니다. 30분 정도 강연을 듣고 질의응답 시간을 갖겠습니다.

차 박사님, IGE 포럼에 오신 것을 다시 한번 환영합니다.

빅터 차 박사: 이사장님, 따뜻한 환영사에 진심으로 감사드립니다. 다시 한 번 IGE 웨비나에서 여러분과 함께하게 되어 기쁩니다. 모두 새해 복 많이 받으시길 바랍니다.

먼저 저는 제가 이 웨비나의 주제를 접하고 생각한 일곱 개의 주요 현안(키워드)에 대해 말씀을 드리는 것으로 오늘 강연을 시작하고자 합니다. 제 생각에는 한국, 트럼프와 한미 동맹, 그리고 북한과 관련된 이 주제들이 오늘 저희 논의를 위해 충분한 기초를 제공해줄 것이라 생각합니다.

첫 번째 주제는 모두가 잘 아시는 바와 같이 장기화되고 있는 한국 내의 정치적 불안정과 지도력 공백입니다. 이는 모든 문제에 영향을 미칠 수 있는 중요한 요소입니다. 이는 경제적, 정치적 측면 모두에 불행한 상황이지만, 그 영향이 최소화되기를 희망합니다. 탄핵국면이 한국에서 처음은 아니기 때문에 과거 위기 관리와 회복의 경험이 저뿐만 아니라 많은 이들로 하여금 이 같은 희망을 갖게 한다고 봅니다. 최근 역사에서 보면 2004년과 2016년에 두 번의 정치적 위기가 있었으며, 결과는 달랐지만 결국 정치와 경제는 회복되었습니다. 이에 많은 정부 기관과 학계를 비롯한 관련 전문가들은 이와 같은 경험을 기반으로 이번에도 회복을 기대하고 있습니다.

하지만 경제적인 측면에서는 우려가 있습니다. 현재로서는 여름 초중반까지는 정치적 혼란이 해결될 것이라는 공감대가 있는 듯한데요, 만약 이때까지 해결되지 않는다면 보다 광범위하고 장기적인 경제적 영향을 입게 될 수 있습니다. 그 이유는 2004년과 2016년의 경우 위기가 있었지만, 경제 회복에 도움이 된 중요한 변수들이 있었습니다.

2004년, 노무현 대통령의 탄핵 이후 경제적 영향을 최소화했던 주요 요인 중 하나는 중국의 경제 성장률이 두 자릿수였다는 점입니다. 중국은 세계무역기구(WTO)에 가입한 후 빠른 경제 성장을 이룩했고, 이는 한국 경제의 빠른 회복에 큰 도움이 되었습니다. 2016~2017년, 박근혜 대통령 탄핵 당시에도 경제적 영향이 있었지만, 반도체 수출 호조가 이를 상쇄시켰습니다. 반도체 산업의 성장은 당시 한국 경제에 큰 도움이 되었고, 정치적 위기에도 경제적 타격은 적었습니다.

하지만 2025년의 경우, 상황이 달라질 수 있습니다. 중국은 2004년과 같은 속도의 경제 성장세를 보이지 않으며, 반도체 부문 수출도 2016년, 2017년의 수준에는 미치지 못하는 상황입니다. 또한, 현재 유럽에서는 전쟁이 진행 중이고, 중동에서는 또 다른 전쟁이 일어날 가능성이 있습니다. 트럼프 행정부의 경제 정책과 그가 동맹국들에게 어떤 경제적 조치를 취할지에 대한 불확실성도 존재합니다. 따라서 한국의 정치적 위기가 올해 여름까지 해결되지 못한다면 경제 회복을 어렵게 만들 수 있습니다.

장기적인 위기는 한국이 트럼프 행정부와의 관계에서 어려움을 겪을 수 있는 상황을 만들기도 합니다. 현재까지 트럼프와 일론 머스크를 만난 한국의 주요 인물은 민간 부문에서만 나타났습니다. 신세계 그룹의 CEO가 트럼프 주니어의 초청으로 마라라고를 방문했으며, 또 다른 경제 그룹의 CEO들도 트럼프의 취임식에 초대받았습니다. 그런데 정작 한국 정부는 정치적 공백 상태에 있어 트럼프 대통령이 취임하고 나면 대응에 어려움이 있을 수 있습니다. 이에 대해서는 잠시 후 좀 더 자세히 설명드리겠습니다.

두 번째 주요 주제는 북한입니다. 북한은 지속적인 안보 위협을 가하고 있으며, 이 위협은 한국 내 정치적 불안정이 지속될 경우 더욱 심화될 수 있습니다. 바이든 행정부 하에서 북한은 162회의 도발을 감행했으며, 그 중 90회는 미사일 발사, 32회는 풍선 발사였습니다. 이는 1953년 이후 어느 미 행정부 하에서 보다도 가장 많은 도발 사례입니다. 트럼프 1기 행정부 당시에는 41회의 도발이 있었으며, 그 중 35회는 미사일 시험, 1회는 핵실험, 나머지 5회는 기타 도발이었습니다. 트럼프와 한국 행정부는 지금보다 더 공격적이고 제어되지 않는 북한을 상대하고 있습니다.

특히 우리는 북한의 오판 가능성에 대해 우려하고 있습니다. 한국의 정치적 위기가 장기화되면 북한이 이를 기회로 삼아 도발할 가능성도 커집니다. 예를 들어, 북한은 최근 1월 6일 IRBM을 발사하며 이를 극초음속 미사일이라고 주장했습니다. 이는 작년 11월 4일 단거리 탄도미사일 발사 후 2025년 첫 번째 시험발사였으며, 트럼프 취임을 앞두고 이루어진 도발이었습니다. 북한은 새로운 미국 행정부 출범 시 마다 이를 계기로 도발을 하려는 경향이 있습니다. 오바마 행정부 출범 당시에는 핵실험을, 트럼프 행정부 출범 당시에도 열핵실험을 감행한 바 있습니다. 바이든 행정부 출범 첫해가 유일하게 예외였는데, 그 당시 북한은 아무런 행동을 취하지 않았습니다. 하지만 이는 당시 북한이 COVID-19 봉쇄 조치에 있었기 때문으로 보이며, 이로 인해 아무것도 할 수 없었던 것으로 생각됩니다. 그러나 북한은 지난 몇 년 동안 취한 모든 조치를 통해 그 예외적인 부분을 충분히 만회했다고 할 수 있습니다.

러시아-북한 간의 동맹관계 강화는 북한에 그들이 시연하고자 하는 새로운 미사일 기술을 제공할 수 있습니다. 새로운 잠수함 기술이 포함될 가능성도 있습니다. 더불어, 양측 간 체결된 새로운 안보 조약은 북한이 지나치게 자신감을 느끼게 할 수 있습니다.

물론 동시에 북한이 더 신중할 수도 있습니다. 만약 북한이 도발을 감행할 경우 비상계엄 포고문에 반국가적 친북 활동과 관련 내용이 기재되고 관련 내용이 비상계엄 당시 언급된 만큼 윤 정부의 계엄령에 정당성을 부여할 수 있고 불필요한 갈등의 격화는 북한에 불리할 수 있기 때문입니다. 특히 북한이 러-우 전쟁에 러시아를 지원하기 위해 군을 파병하고, 동시에 남북을 연결하는 도로를 파괴하는 등 방어적 조치를 취하고 있는 때인 만큼 신중할 수 있습니다.

세 번째 주요 주제는 트럼프 행정부와 관련된 문제입니다. 특히 트럼프가 한미방위분담특별협정(SMA) 및 방위비 분담금 문제에 어떻게 대응할지가 우려되며 이는 가장 중요한 부분입니다. 현재의 SMA 협정, 즉 제12차 SMA 협정은 2026년부터 2030년까지를 다루고 있습니다. 미국과 한국은 방위비 분담의 첫해인 2026년에 10억 달러를 조금 넘는 금액을 설정했으며, 이는 2025년 대비 8.3% 증가한 액수입니다. 또한 여러분이 잘 아시다시피, 바이든 행정부는 SMA가 두 해도 더 남아 있음에도 불구하고 동맹의 긴장과 합의 부족을 피하려는 선제적 조치로 SMA를 조기에 갱신하자고 제안한 바 있습니다. 이는 첫 번째 트럼프 행정부 시절에 우리가 경험한 상황과 유사한 상황을 방지하려는 노력의 일환이었습니다.

하지만 이제 트럼프가 다시 취임하게 되면, 그가 협정을 파기하거나 철회하거나 재협상을 압박할 가능성이 우려됩니다. 제 추측으로는, 이 협정 재협상 당시 트럼프는 캠페인에 집중하고 있었기 때문에 이 문제에 큰 관심을 두지 않았을 것으로 보입니다. 하지만 아시는 분들도 계시듯이, 트럼프는 지난 10월 기자회견에서 한국이 방위비 분담금으로 매년 100억 달러를 지불해야 한다고 말한 바 있습니다.

미군 철수와 관련된 우려도 있습니다. 트럼프는 많은 동맹국들이 공짜로 미국으로부터 안보를 제공받고 있다고 보고 있고, 이로 인한 비용으로 무역적자가 발생하고 있다고 생각합니다.

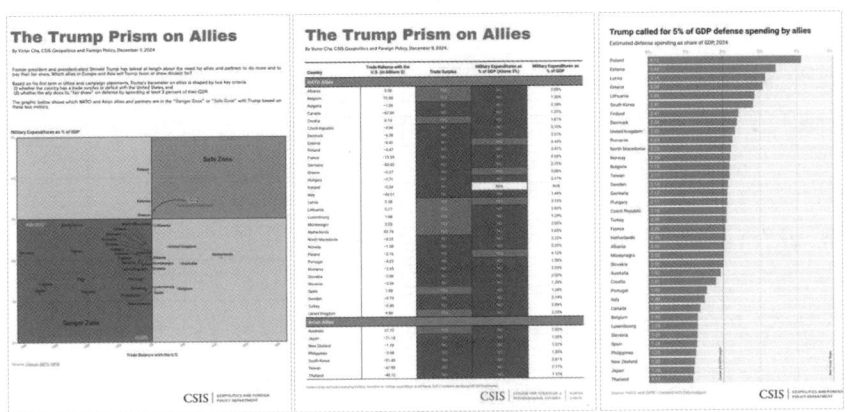

이 슬라이드는 트럼프가 동맹국과 파트너를 어떻게 보는지를 잘 요약한 것입니다. 그는 기본적으로 두 가지 축을 기준으로 동맹국을 평가합니다.

첫 번째 축은 무역과 관련이 있습니다. 동맹국이나 파트너가 미국과의 무역에서 흑자를 내는지 적자를 내는지에 관한 것입니다. 두 번째 축은 국방비 지출 관련으로, 상대국이 충분한 국방비를 지출하는지에 대한 것입니다. 여기서 '충분한'이란 GDP의 3%를 국방비로 지출하는 것을 의미합니다. 우리는 이 두 축을 선택한 이유는 트럼프가 항상 동맹국과 파트너에 대해 이야기할 때, 그들이 무역에서 자신을 속이고 있으며 미국이 모두의 국방을 책임지고 있다는 것을 언급해왔기 때문입니다. 그는 첫 임기 동안에도 이 점을 여러 번 언급했고, 현재도 계속해서 그렇게 말하고 있습니다. 이 문제는 그가 수십 년 동안 믿어 온 것입니다.

그래서 우리는 모든 NATO 동맹국과 인도-태평양 동맹국 및 파트너들을 이 두 축을 기준으로 분석해 보았습니다. 보시다시피, 트럼프의 시각에서 보면 대부분의 NATO 동맹국과 인도-태평양 파트너들이 하나 또는 두 가지 문제에서 부족하다고 평가됩니다. 무역 측면에서는 그들이 미국과의 무역에서 흑자를 보고 있고, 국방비 측면에서는 GDP의 3% 미만으로 국방비를 지출하고 있습니다.

트럼프의 기준을 충족하는 유일한 NATO 동맹국은 라트비아이고, 트럼프의 기준을 완전히 벗어나지 않는 유일한 인도-태평양 동맹국은 호주입니다. 호주는 유일하게 미국과 무역 적자를 보고 있는 인도-태평양 동맹국입니다. 한국은 그 외 동맹국들과 마찬가지로 무역 흑자를 보고 있으며, 그 금액은 약 514억 달러로, NATO와 미국 동맹국들 중에서 독일, 일본, 캐나다에 이어 네 번째로 높은 수준입니다.

한국은 트럼프가 한국에서 군대를 철수할 가능성에 대해 우려해왔습니다. 트럼프의 첫 임기 동안에는 미국 의회에서 미군을 한국에 유지해야 한다는 양당의 초당적 합의가 있었기 때문에 이 우려가 어느 정도 해소되었습니다. 하지만 트럼프 2기에는 공화당이 미 의회 상하원 모두의 다수를 차지하는 만큼 이 같은 초당적 합의가 여전히 존재한다고 볼 수 없습니다. 더 나아가, 아마도 가장 중요한 점은 2025년 국가방위법(National Defense Authorization Act)입니다. 이 법에는 이전에 미국 행정부가 한국에서 군을 철수하는 것을 제한하는 조항이 있었습니다. 이는 트럼프 행정부 시절에 포함되었던 조항이었습니다. 그러나 현재는 이 조항이 국가방위법에서 더 이상 포함되지 않았습니다. 트럼프가 한국이나 독일에서 군을 철수하는 등의 조치를 취할 때 이를 제한할 수 있는 의회 차원의 제약이 이제는 사라진 것입니다. 이는 주로 바이든 행정부의 4년 동안 그러한 필요가 없었기 때문이라고 볼 수 있는데, 그러나 이제는 확실히 우려되는 사항이라고 할 수 있습니다.

제가 언급하고 싶은 네 번째 요점은 바로 관세에 대한 우려입니다. 앞서 말했듯이, 트럼프는 한국과 같은 국가를 보고 막대한 무역 흑자를 보며, 동시에 방위비 지출이 낮다는 점을 지적합니다. 미군이 주둔하는 국가의 방위비 지출이 각국 GDP의 3% 수준이 되어야 한다고 했는데, 언젠가는 3%도 충분하지 않다며 5%로 설정해야 한다고 주장한 바 있습니다. 이 경우 어떤 국가도, 인도-태평양 지역의 동맹국이나 NATO 동맹국도 이 숫자를 충족하지 못합니다.

다음주 트럼프가 취임하면 새로운 관세 프로그램을 시행하기 위해 국가 경제 비상사태를 선포할 가능성이 우려됩니다. 이 경우 트럼프는 국제긴급경제권한법(International Emergency Economic Powers Act, IEEPA)을 사용해 새로운 관세 프로그램을 구성할 수 있게 됩니다. 이는 대통령이 국가 비상사태 시 수입을 관리할 수 있도록 일방적으로 권한을 부여하는 법안입니다. 이에 대한 우려는 부분적으로 한국 원화 약세를 초래한 이유 중 하나이기도 합니다.

물론, 이것이 유일한 이유는 아닙니다. 10%의 전방위적인 관세나, IEEPA를 통한 새로운 종류의 관세 체계, 그리고 미국이 전방위적인 관세 대신 특정 기업을 겨냥해 수입 쿼터를 부과할 수 있는 무역법의 또 다른 조항이 실제로 적용될 가능성 등도 있기 때문입니다. 이러한 조치는 아마도 중국의 기업들에 더 많이 적용될 가능성이 있지만 한국도 경계할 수밖에 없는 부분입니다.

다섯 번째 요점은 트럼프 행정부와 북한 간의 관계에서 일어날 수 있는 일들과 관련된 것입니다. 여기에는 몇 가지 세부 사항이 있지만, 이를 세 가지 범주로 나눠서 설명하겠습니다. 첫 번째는 미국이 북한과의 관계에서 군비 통제 패러다임으로 전환하고, CVID(완전하고 검증 가능하며 되돌릴 수 없는 비핵화)를 포기할 가능성에 대한 우려입니다.

2023년 12월에 보고된 바에 따르면, 트럼프는 북한이 핵무기를 보유하는 것을 허용하고, 북한이 수직적 핵 확산, 즉 더 많은 핵무기나 장거리 ICBM을 제조하지 않도록 금융적 인센티브를 제공하는 계획을 고려하고 있다는 보도가 있었습니다. 이는 일종의 군비 통제 협상에 들어가서 북한이 핵무기를 유지하되, 미국에 가장 위협적인 핵무기나 ICBM을 생산하는 것을 중단하는 방식이었습니다. 이는 한국에 매우 우려스러운 상황이 될 수 있지만, 트럼프는 비핵화와 관련된 이전 협상 시도가 실패한 사실을 잘 알고 있을 것입니다. 일부에서는 이것이 그들이 고려하고 있을 수 있는 방안이라고 말하기도 했습니다. 이 점이 바로 다섯 번째 요점입니다.

여섯 번째 점은 디커플링에 대한 우려입니다. 트럼프가 북한이 미국 본토에 위협이 되는 능력 개발을 중단하는 조건으로 부분적인 제재 완화를 제안할 가능성을 배제하지 않을 수 있습니다. 그러나 이는 한반도를 위협하는 능력에 집중하지는 않을 것입니다. 이러한 접근법과 군비 통제 협정은 동맹 내에서 디커플링의 형태가 될 수 있습니다. 이는 미국이 자국의 안보만을 위해 협상하고 동맹국들의 안보는 고려하지 않게 된다는 의미입니다. 또한 북한을 사실상 핵무기 보유국으로 인정하는 효과를 가져오게 되며, 이는 한국에 큰 위협이 될 수 있습니다.

이에 관련된 우려는 미국과 북한 간의 협상에서 '코리아 패싱(Korea passing)'에 대한 문제입니다. 특히 트럼프 행정부가 출범한 지 6개월 이상 지나도록 한국에 기능하는 정부가 없다면, '코리아 패싱'의 가능성이 매우 높아질 것입니다. 만약 한국에 기능하는 정부가 없다면, 한국을 배제하는 상황이 매우 현실적이 될 수 있습니다. 물론, 현 정부는 오늘날 바이든 행정부와의 정기적인 연락을 유지하기 위해 최선을 다하고 있습니다. 조현동 주미대사가 매우 활발히 활동하고 있으며, 국가안보보좌관, 외교부 차관들, 국방부 장관도 모두 매우 적극적으로 활동하고 있습니다.

하지만, 미국 내 모든 사람들, 특히 새로운 트럼프 행정부는 현재의 바이든 정부와는 다르게 한국의 새로운 정부와 협력해야 한다는 사실을 잘 알고 있습니다. 개인적으로 그런 일이 없기를 바라지만, 상황이 더 어려워질 것으로 보입니다. 바이든 행정부는 한국 측과 계속해서 많은 회의를 진행하며 지속성을 보장하려는 자세를 매우 적극적으로 취해왔지만, 트럼프 2기 행정부는 한국에 새로운 정부가 들어설 때까지 이러한 회의에 관심을 두지 않을 가능성이 커 보이며 이점이 우려됩니다.

특히 트럼프가 북한과의 잠재적인 "조기 협상"에 나설 가능성을 경계해야 합니다. 북한의 도발이 계속해서 증가한다면, 트럼프에 이 문제를 가능한 한 빨리 해결하라는 압박이 있을 수 있습니다. 물론, 트럼프가 당장은 세금 감면, 국경 문제, 이민 문제와 같은 국내 문제와 국제적으로는 가자 지구의 평화 정착과 우크라이나 전쟁에 집중할 가능성이 큽니다.

하지만 트럼프가 북한과의 조기 협상에 나설 이유도 무시할 수 없습니다. 첫째, 트럼프는 매우 자신감 있는 인물이며, 김정은과 오랫동안 연락을 유지해왔다는 점이 주된 이유입니다. 북한과의 협상에서 자신감을 느낄 수 있을 것이며, 이는 그가 조기에 협상에 나설 수 있는 요인으로 작용할 수 있습니다.

둘째, 트럼프를 제지할 고위 관리들의 부재입니다. 트럼프의 첫 번째 임기 동안에는 H.R. 맥마스터, 존 볼턴, 제임스 매티스와 같은 사람들, 즉 그의 국가안보보좌관들이 있었고, 이들은 트럼프가 너무 위험하거나 지나치게 모험적인 일을 하지 않도록 제지하려 했습니다. 그러나 트럼프의 두 번째 임기에서 보면, 그의 주요 임명 기준은 이들이 주류 공화당 당론과 성향에 부합하는지가 아니라, 트럼프에게 100% 충성하는지를 기준으로 삼고 있다는 점입니다. 특히 국방장관과 국가정보국장 후보자 임명에서, 또는 법무장관 임명에서, 그는 트럼프에게 극도로 충성하는 사람들을 임명하고 있다는 것이 분명히 보였습니다. 이 같은 여건에서는 트럼프에 대한 내부적인 제약은 부족할 가능성이 큽니다.

세 번째 이유는 오히려 반대로 트럼프가 새로운 정부가 들어서기 전에 한국과의 동맹에서 더 나은 레버리지를 확보하기 위해 북한과의 조기 협상을 시도할 수 있다는 점입니다. 다시 말해, 그는 SMA 재협상에서 더 나은 레버리지를 얻거나, 군 철수 또는 평화 조약과 같은 문제를 다룰 때 더 나은 위치에 서기 위해 북한과의 조기 협상을 추구할 수 있습니다. 이러한 모든 상황은 매우 다르고 패러다임을 바꾸는 시나리오들입니다.

일곱 번째 요점은 트럼프 2기 행정부와 관련하여 여러 가지 우려해야 할 사항들이 있지만, 그럼에도 불구하고 트럼프가 즉각적으로 조기 협상에 나설 가능성을 제약할 수 있는 몇 가지 요인들이 있다는 점입니다.

첫 번째 제약 요인은 제가 이미 언급한 바와 같이, 트럼프가 다른 여러 중요한 이슈들에 집중해야 하므로 북한 문제에 우선순위를 두기 어려울 수 있다는 점입니다. 다시 말해, 우크라이나 전쟁, 관세, 가자 지구 전쟁, 국경 문제, 이민 문제 등 여러 중요한 사안들이 그의 초점이 될 것이기 때문에, 북한과의 협상에 집중할 시간이 부족할 가능성이 큽니다. 많은 초기 행정명령이 이러한 문제들에 초점을 맞출 것 같고, 북한과의 협상은 많은 시간과 에너지를 요구하는 작업이기 때문에 그가 즉시 이를 진행할 시간이 부족할 수 있습니다.

두 번째 제약 요인은 제가 앞서 언급한 것과는 반대되는 점인데, 트럼프는 김정은과 대화하고 협상하는 데 자신감을 가지고 있을 수 있지만, 동시에 김정은을 신뢰하지 않을 수도 있다는 점입니다. 이는 2018년 싱가포르 회담에서 합의를 본 것으로 생각했으나 이후 2019년 하노이 회담이 결렬되며 실패로 끝난 점, 이후 판문점 회담 이후 더 이상의 진전이 없었던 사실에 근거한 것입니다.

세 번째 이유는 미국보다는 북한과 러시아의 관계에 더 관련이 있습니다. 현재 북한과 러시아의 관계는 매우 강하게 발전하고 있습니다. 이는 냉전 시기 두 나라가 공유했던 안보 보장과 동맹을 재구성하는 형태입니다. 북한은 현재 러시아로부터 식량, 연료, 의약품 등 많은 것을 받고 있으며, 이러한 관계가 더욱 커지면서 북한은 미국과 협상할 필요성을 덜 느낄 수 있습니다. 북한은 러시아와의 큰 관계 때문에 미국과 협상할 동기를 덜 느낄 수도 있습니다.

2017~2018년 북한의 상황은 달랐습니다. 그때는 러시아와 강한 관계가 없었고, 중국과도 강한 관계를 맺고 있지 않았기 때문에 미국과 협상이 필요하다고 생각했을 수 있습니다. 그러나 현재 북한은 러시아와 매우 강한 관계를 맺고 있으며, 중국은 러시아와의 관계로 인해 북한과의 관계를 강화하려고 노력하고 있습니다. 이로 인해 북한은 적어도 당분간 트럼프와 협상할 필요성을 느끼지 않을 수 있습니다. 이것이 바로 조기 협상에 제약을 둘 수 있는 세 번째 이유입니다.

이 모든 점을 고려할 때, 우리는 새로운 미국 대통령의 취임을 앞두고, 한국 내 정치 상황이 어떻게 전개되는지 지켜보며 많은 것을 생각할 필요가 있습니다.

그런데, 제 입장에서는 워싱턴 DC에서 요즘 많이 받는 질문들이 북한이나 트럼프 행정부가 무엇을 할 것 인지와는 전혀 관련이 없습니다. 대부분 질문은 현재 한국에서 일어나고 있는 일들과 정치적 위기가 얼마나 빨리 해결될 것인지에 관한 것입니다. 오늘날 세계의 더 넓은 맥락 하에 많은 글로벌 거버넌스와 자유주의 기반의 기관들이 어려움을 겪고 있는 상황에서 윤 대통령이 G7과 NATO에 참여하고 우크라이나에 지원을 제공하는 등 국제적으로 한국의 글로벌 존재감을 높이고 있던 시점이었던 만큼 대내적 이슈를 불문하고 해외에서는 윤 대통령에 대한 긍정적인 평가가 많았습니다. 일본, 동남아시아, 유럽 전역에서 그런 이야기를 들었습니다. 한국이 세계 12~13위 경제 대국으로서 정치적, 경제적으로 국제문제에 나서고 있다는 점에 대해서는 많은 인정을 받은 바 있었습니다.

이러한 이유로 현재 한국에서 일어나고 있는 일들에 큰 관심이 집중되고 있으며, 저는 이 문제가 머지않아 해결되기를 바랍니다. 경청해 주셔서 대단히 감사합니다.

전광우 이사장: 차 박사님, 훌륭한 강연 감사합니다. 트럼프 2기 행정부가 다음 출범하는 만큼 우리는 지금 매우 중요한 시기에 직면해 있습니다. 설상가상으로 한국의 내부 정치 상황이 그 어느 때보다 불안정하고 걱정스러운 상황이기도 합니다. 하지만

박사님께서 말씀하신 대로 한국은 과거 경제적, 정치적 위기 속에서도 뛰어난 회복력을 보여주었습니다. 이번에도 당면한 혼란에 잘 대처해서 한국의 뛰어난 복원력을 다시 한 번 입증할 수 있기를 기대합니다.

이제 토론 및 질의응답 시간 세션을 시작하겠습니다. 오늘은 특별히 세 분의 저명한 분들을 모셨는데요. 먼저 영원무역 그룹의 성기학 회장님께서 함께해 주시고 계십니다. 현재 출장 중이신 베트남에서 접속하고 계십니다. 그리고 주미한국대사를 지내신 안호영 대사님을 모셨습니다. 주한유럽상공회의소(ECCK) 회장이신 필립 반 후프 대표님께서는 한국과 동아시아 현안에 대한 해외 시각을 공유해주시기 위해 참석하셨습니다.

그럼 먼저 성기학 회장님의 말씀을 듣겠습니다. 안녕하세요, 회장님.

성기학 회장: 차 박사님, 이번 모임에 참석하게 되어 매우 기쁘며, 현 상황에 대해 상세히 설명해 주셔서 진심으로 감사드립니다.

저는 현재 한국의 대외적 이슈보다도 한국 내의 여러 문제에 대해 더 큰 우려를 가지고 있습니다. 최근 정치적인 상황이 변화하면서, 일부 국민들 사이에서는 현 정부의 정책과 관련된 논의가 활발히 이루어지고 있으며, 이에 대한 관심이 커지고 있는 상황입니다. 특히, 현 정부 지도자에 대한 관심도 급격히 상승하고 있는 것으로 보입니다. 현재 제가 보고 있는 국내 상황이 이렇습니다.

하지만 북한의 압박은 이전보다 훨씬 약해진 느낌을 받습니다. 물론, 러시아와 북한의 동맹이 강화되고 이에 러시아가 북한의 군사적 역량을 강화할 만한 기술적 지원을 할 가능성이 있지만, 이를 제외하면 북한의 압박이 이전보다는 많이 줄어들었다고 느껴집니다.

단, 중국은 여전히 중요한 영향력을 미치고 있으며, 이는 우리가 반드시 주의 깊게 살펴야 할 문제입니다. 경제적인 관점에서 보면, 중국의 과잉 공급이 한국 및 주변 국가들의 산업에 큰 타격을 주고 있습니다. 이로 인해 여러 산업들이 붕괴되고 있는 상황인 만큼 이에 대해 면밀히 검토하고 우리 산업들을 보호할 방법을 모색해야 합니다.

불행히도 이 같은 중요한 시점에 한국의 정치적인 불확실성이 커져서 정부에 대한 국민들의 신뢰에 영향을 미칠 수 있습니다.

차 박사님, 다시 한번 오늘 강연에 감사의 말씀을 드립니다. 여러 가지 논의할 점들이 많아서 기회가 된다면 직접 만나 뵙고 현 상황에 대해 더 깊이 이해할 수 있는 시간을 갖고자 합니다. 대단히 감사합니다.

전광우 이사장: 감사합니다. 다음으로, 안호영 대사님을 모시겠습니다. 워낙 잘 알려지신 분인만큼 자세한 소개말씀은 생략하도록 하겠습니다. 대사님, 안녕하세요?

안호영 대사: 초청해 주셔서 감사합니다 이사장님. 그리고 차 박사님, 바쁜 일정 중에도 시간을 내어 훌륭한 강연을 해 주셔서 감사합니다. 우리가 당면한 현안들에 대해 7가지 요점들을 잘 정리해 주셔서 매우 인상 깊었고, 다시 한 번 감사드립니다. 저는 특히 그 중 5번과 6번에 대해 질문을 드리고 싶습니다.

5번에서는 트럼프 행정부가 북한 핵 문제의 목표를 비핵화에서 군비 통제로 전환할 가능성에 대해 말씀하셨고, 6번에서는 미국과 한국의 전략적 이해관계를 분리할 가능성에 대해 언급하셨습니다. 이 두 가지를 듣고 제 머릿속에 두 가지 질문이 떠올랐습니다.

첫 번째는 이러한 변화가 실제로 발생할 가능성이 얼마나 높다고 보시는지 궁금합니다. 우리 모두 잘 알고 있듯이, 북한의 핵 문제는 현재 트럼프의 신 정부의 인수인계위원회에서 심도 깊게 논의되고 있으며, 이 과정은 시간이 더 걸릴 것으로 예상됩니다. 그렇다면 트럼프 행정부 하에서 비핵화에서 군비 통제로 목표가 전환되고, 미국과 한국의 전략적 이해관계가 분리될 가능성은 실제로 얼마나 높은지에 대해 어떻게 보시나요?

두 번째 질문은, 만약 이런 일이 실제로 발생한다면, 즉 비핵화에서 군비 통제로 목표가 변경되고, 미국과 한국 간의 전략적 이해관계가 분리된다면, 그로 인한 한국에 대한 영향은 매우 클 것인 만큼 이와 관련된 질문들입니다. 이는 한국에 전혀 다른 지정학적, 지경학적 상황을 초래할 수 있습니다. 그런 상황에서는 앞서 언급 하신 것처럼 중국의 반응이 매우 중요하다고 생각합니다.

제가 보기에는 중국은 트럼프의 재집권으로 미국과 그 동맹국들 간의 동맹 관계가 약화될 가능성이 높아짐에 따라 중국에게 새로운 기회를 제공할 수 있다는 점을 긍정적으로 생각할 수도 있을 듯 합니다. 트럼프 행정부가 비핵화에서 군비 통제로 초점을 전환하는 상황이 바로 그런 기회를 만들 수 있을 것입니다. 동시에, 한국에서는 독자적인 핵무장에 대한 압박이 거세질 수 있다는 점도 고려해야 합니다. 이러한 여러 가지 질문들이 제 머릿속에 떠오르고 있습니다.

이 밖에, 차 박사님께서 말씀하신 제약 요소 관련하여 저도 두 가지 추가적인 제약 요소가 떠올랐습니다.

첫 번째는 의회의 역할입니다. 최근 상원 군사위원회 위원장으로 로저 위커 의원, 외교위원회 위원장으로 제임스 리시 의원이 임명되었는데요, 이들 두 의원이 동맹국과 한국, 그리고 북한의 핵 문제에 대해 어떤 입장을 가지고 있는지 잘 아실 것입니다. 저는 또한 하원에서도 무기통제위원회와 외교위원회의 리더십이 비슷한 성향을 가진 인물들일 가능성이 크다고 생각합니다. 이는 트럼프 1기에서도 중요한 제약 요소로 작용했던 부분이었고, 트럼프 2기에서도 여전히 큰 제약 요소가 될 수 있을 것입니다.

두 번째 제약 요소는 바로 차 박사님 본인이십니다. 차 박사님께서는 북한 문제를 다루고 있는 트럼프 행정부 내 인물들에게 중요한 현실적인 조언을 하실 수 있는 중요한 위치에 계십니다.

마지막으로 한 가지 더 말씀드리고자 합니다. 박사님의 말씀을 듣고, 2017년 초 트럼프 행정부 초기 시절이 떠올랐습니다. 그 당시 2월에는 매티스 국방장관이 한국을 방문했으며, 3월에는 틸러슨 국무장관, 4월에는 펜스 부통령이 한국을 방문했습니다. 당시 한국은 황교안 권한대행이 대통령 직무를 대행하고 있었지만, 그럼에도 불구하고 트럼프 행정부의 고위 인사들이 매우 바쁜 일정 속에서도 한국을 방문한 것은 매우 의미 있는 일이었습니다. 이는 트럼프 행정부가 한국에 대해 강력한 동맹 의지를 보이려는 의도가 있었던 것으로 해석됩니다. 여기서 제 발언을 마치겠습니다. 다시 한 번 감사드립니다.

빅터 차 박사: 성기학 회장님과 안호영 대사님, 두 분의 훌륭한 말씀에 대해 감사드립니다. 이런 높은 수준의 그룹에서 발표자가 기업 CEO나 대사로부터 의견을 듣는 것은 정말 드문 일입니다. IGE 포럼에서만 가능한 일입니다.

시간이 부족한 점을 감안하여, 최대한 간결하게 답변을 드리겠습니다.

첫 번째로, 성 회장님께서 말씀하신 것처럼 러시아 총리가 지금 베트남에 있다는 점은 매우 흥미롭습니다. 전 세계적으로 잘 보도되지 않았지만, 푸틴이 베트남과 관련하여 추구하는 전략은 분명히 존재합니다. 물론 푸틴은 평양을 방문할 때 베트남에도 방문했습니다. 저는 푸틴이 북한과 베트남을 아시아에서 중국의 입지를 재구축하기 위한 중요한 두 축으로 보고 있다고 생각합니다. 이는 미국과 중국 모두에게 불안감을 초래하는 방식으로 이뤄질 것으로 봅니다. 푸틴이 북한과 베트남을 선택한 이유는 이 두 나라가 미국과 아시아에서 중국의 전통적인 영향력을 흔들 수 있는 가능성이 크기 때문입니다. 이는 푸틴의 전략적인 의도가 담긴 진지한 노력이라고 볼 수 있습니다.

다음으로, 여당인 국민의 힘의 최근 지지율 상승에 대해서는 현재 그 지지율이 40포인트에 달하고 민주당과 오차범위 내에 있다는 보도를 읽었습니다. 이는 많은 미국인들이 예상하지 못한 일입니다. 이 사실이 윤 대통령의 향후 운명에 어떤 영향을 미칠지는 알 수 없지만, 미국의 관점에서 이는 중요한 신호로 해석됩니다. 한국 국민들이 12월 3일 윤 대통령의 행보에 대해 상반된 의견을 가질 수 있겠지만, 미국에서는 대체로 한국 국민들이 여당과 윤 대통령의 외교 정책에 대해 긍정적인 반응을 보였다고 이해하고 있습니다. 이는 매우 중요한 메시지를 전달하는 것입니다.

북한과의 협상에서 디커플링되는 문제와 관련하여, 저는 이를 "트럼프가 더 쉬운 거래를 원하는지, 아니면 더 어려운 거래를 원할지"라는 관점에서 생각해 봅니다. 어려운 거래는 CVID(완전하고 검증 가능하며 불가역적인 핵 폐기)와 관련된 사항들입니다. 이 거래는 핵무기, 장거리 탄도 미사일, 단거리 탄도 미사일을 포함한 복잡한 문제들을 해결하는 것을 목표로 합니다. 반면, 쉬운 거래는 핵 실험과 미사일 실험(특히 장거리 미사일 시험)을 중단시키는 수준에 그치며, 그 외의 문제는 크게 신경 쓰지 않는 형태입니다.

저는 트럼프가 훨씬 더 쉬운 거래를 선호하는 경향이 있다고 생각합니다. 첫 임기 동안, 일본의 아베 총리와 다른 사람들이 단거리 미사일 실험에 대해 언급했을 때, 그는 "단거리 미사일에 신경 쓰지 않는다. 모두가 가지고 있다"라고 말한 바 있습니다. 이는 좋은 신호가 아닙니다.

중국과 관련해서는, 저는 트럼프 행정부 하에서 중국이 기회가 있을 것으로 보고 있다고 생각합니다. 비록 바이든 행정부가 양자 동맹 관계에서 상당한 진전을 이루었지만, 중국은 트럼프가 이를 되돌릴 가능성이 높다고 보고 있습니다. 캠프 데이비드, AUKUS(오스트리아-영국-미국 3자 방위 파트너쉽), IPEF(인도-태평양 경제 프레임워크), 쿼드 등에서 실질적인 진전이 있었지만, 트럼프는 이러한 부분에 큰 신경을 쓰지 않을 것이라고 보기에, 중국은 이를 역으로 이용할 수 있을 것으로 보고 있습니다.

의회와 같은 제약 요소들에 대해 말씀드리자면, 트럼프의 행보에 제약을 시도할 수 있는 사람들이 존재한다고 생각합니다. 예를 들어, 군대 철수를 반대하는 사람들이 있을 것이고, 알렉스 웡 국가안보부보좌관과 이반 카나파시 국가안보회의 고위 이사와 같은 사람들이 외교 정책에서 중요한 역할을 맡고 있습니다. 다만, 결국 정책을 만드는 것은 트럼프 자신이기 때문에, 이들은 트럼프의 정책을 따르는 상황이 될 것입니다.

2017년과 2018년 초, 틸러슨 국무장관과 펜스 부통령이 한국을 방문한 당시 상황에 대해 말씀드리면, 그때의 상황은 두 가지 측면에서 작금의 상황과는 달랐다고 봅니다. 첫 번째는, 틸러슨과 다른 고위 인사들의 방문이 트럼프 행정부 내부의 외교 정책을 둘러싼 경쟁의 일환이었다는 점입니다. 당시, 누가 외교 정책을 주도할지를 놓고 치열한 논쟁이 있었으며, 이는 맥마스터의 책에서 확인할 수 있습니다. 맥마스터와 틸러슨은 그 문제를 놓고 격렬한 의견 충돌을 벌인 바 있습니다.

두 번째는, 당시 북한의 도발이 계속되었기 때문에 한국과의 강력한 동맹을 재확인하고자 했던 의도가 있었다는 점입니다. 당시 트럼프는 북한 문제를 어떻게 처리해야 할지 몰랐고, 그 시점에서 최선의 선택은 동맹국인 한국과의 강한 연대를 보여주는 것이었기 때문에 고위 인사들이 한국을 방문했던 것입니다. 하지만 이번에는 트럼프가 북한 문제를 다루는 방법을 알고 있습니다. 이제 그는 북한 문제에 대해 더 이상 걱정하지 않으며 외교 정책의 주도권을 트럼프가 쥐고 있기 때문에, 그와 관련된 측근들의 내부적인 논란은 발생하지 않을 것입니다. 이것이 제가 코리아 패싱을 더욱 우려하는 이유입니다.

전광우 이사장: 답변 감사합니다. 이제 세 번째 토론자 필립 반 후프 회장님을 모시겠습니다. 주한유럽상공회의소(ECCK) 회장이자 ING 한국 지사장을 맡고 계십니다. 필립 회장님, 말씀 부탁드립니다.

필립 반 후프 회장: 이사장님, 친절한 소개 감사드립니다. 차 교수님, 성 회장님, 안 대사님께도 감사드립니다. 저는 앞서 두분께서 중요한 말씀을 해 주셨기 때문에 이와는 조금 다른 관점에서 좀더 논점을 확장해서 말씀드리도록 하겠습니다.

첫째, 차 박사님께서 여러 차례 브뤼셀을 방문하시고 유럽이 APEC과의 연계를 인식하게 되었다고 느끼셨다고 말씀하신 부분에 깊이 공감합니다. 지난해 10월 유럽연합 주재 한국대사이신 유정현 대사님과의 만남은 제게 유럽이 처한 상황을 이해하는 중요한 기회였습니다. 특히 유럽연합의 여러 부서를 방문하면서, 유럽이 북대서양의 안정뿐만 아니라 북태평양의 안정 없이는 전 세계적인 안정이 불가능하다는 점을 깊이 인식하고 있다는 사실을 실감할 수 있었습니다. 이는 이전 일본 총리님의 말씀을 다시 한번 떠올리게 합니다. 또한, 일본 총리가 오는 6월 마드리드에서 열리는 NATO 정상 회담에 초청받은 것도 매우 중요한 의미가 있다고 생각합니다. 유럽은 분명히 북태평양의 안정이 중요하다는 사실을 인지하고 있습니다.

둘째, 저는 ECCK 회장으로서 최근 한 달 동안 우리가 한국 정부의 여러 주요 인사들과 만날 수 있었다는 것입니다. 최상목 대통령권한대행, 경제부총리, 산업통상자원부 장관을 두 차례 만나 뵈었고, 서울시장, 경기도지사, 금융위원장 등 주요 인사들과도 만남을 가졌습니다. 이와 같은 일은 다른 어떤 나라에서도 경험하기 힘든 일입니다. 어느 나라에서도 외국인 투자자들을 이렇게 세심하게 배려하지 않습니다. 주한미국상공회의소를 비롯한 다른 주요 외국 상공회의소들까지 포함하여 우리가 전달받은 메시지는 매우 강력한 것이었습니다. 우리는 한국의 민주적 시스템이 보여준 회복력과, 우리 회원들이 평상시처럼 비즈니스를 이어가는 모습을 지켜보았습니다.

제 간단한 의견이었습니다만, 저는 이 점을 여러분과 반드시 공유하고 싶었습니다. 한국에 대한 미디어의 이미지는 때때로 다르게 전달될 수 있기 때문입니다. 저는 외국 기업 자회사가 본사에 제출하는 보고서가 실제로는 더 중요한 경우가 많다는 점을 대통령권한대행께 항상 말씀드려왔습니다. 한국에 대한 외국인 투자자들의 신뢰와 판단에 있어서는 평상시 한국 내 외국계 자회사들의 비즈니스 운영에 대한 보고서가 매우 중요한 의미를 갖는다는 점을 강조하고 싶습니다.

이제 질문을 드리고자 합니다. 한국과 미국 간의 중요한 동맹 관계에 대한 우려를 모두 들었습니다. 그런데 조금 다른 시각에서 접근해 보자면, 미국은 동맹국 없이 어떤 모습일까요? 제 생각에 미국은 본질적으로 해양 강국입니다. 미국은 북대서양에 접근할 필요가 있으며, 오늘날 특히 북태평양에 대한 접근이 더욱 중요한 상황입니다. 이를 위해서는 대서양과 태평양 건너편에 강력한 동맹국들이 필요합니다. 너무 도발적인 질문이 되지 않기를 바랍니다.

빅터 차 박사: 필립 회장님, 훌륭한 코멘트와 질문에 감사드립니다. '북대서양의 안정은 북태평양의 안정 없이는 이루어질 수 없다'는 말씀에 전적으로 동의합니다. 이 표현은 매우 탁월하며, 현재의 논의와 협력 수준을 잘 요약하고 있다고 생각합니다.

또한 브뤼셀에 갈 때마다, 유럽에서 이루어지고 있는 북태평양 안보에 관한 논의가 지금은 워싱턴 D.C.에서 우리가 나누는 논의와 비견될 정도로 깊이가 있다고 느낍니다. 5년 전에는 이런 상황이 아니었지만, 지금은 확실히 그렇습니다. NATO에서 북태평양과 일본, 한국 문제를 담당하는 인력들이 매우 우수한 수준을 자랑합니다. 정책의 수준은 결국 사람에 달려 있으며, 좋은 인재가 없으면 좋은 정책도 나오지 않습니다. 다행히도 이 문제에 대해 뛰어난 인재들이 활동하고 있습니다.

두 번째로, 탄핵정국 속 권한대행체제의 한국 정부가 한국내에서 활동하는 주요 유럽 및 미국 비즈니스 커뮤니티에 '비즈니스가 평상시처럼 진행되고 있다'는 메시지를 전하고 있다는 소식을 듣게 되어 매우 기쁩니다. 이는 매우 중요한 메시지입니다. 비상계엄 이후 CSIS에서 전경련과 함께 워싱턴 D.C.에서 한 행사를 주최하게 되었는데, 당시 미국상공회의소는 한국의 비상상황을 이유로 전경련의 방문을 연기해야 할 것인가를 고민했지만, 당시 많은 사람들이 '아니다, 그래서는 안 된다. 비즈니스가 평상시처럼 이루어지고 있다는 모습을 보여줘야 한다'고 말했습니다. 한국의 기업인들은 미국이 트럼프 대통령 하에서 어떻게 될 것인지에 대해 듣고 싶어하고, 미국의 기업인들도 한국에서 발생하고 있는 상황에 대해 알아야 하기 때문에 양측은 명확한 대화 통로를 유지해야 합니다. 이는 매우 중요한 일입니다. 그래서 저는 '비즈니스가 평상시처럼 이루어진다'는 메시지를 적극적으로 주고받는 것에 전적으로 동의합니다.

다음으로, 미국이 동맹국을 필요로 하지 않느냐는 질문에 대해, 저는 100% 동의합니다. 수출 통제, 전략적 경쟁, 러시아, 우크라이나, 중국, 북한, 이란 등의 문제에서 미국은 동맹국과 파트너가 절실히 필요합니다. 저는 이 의견에 완전히 동의합니다. 트럼프 행정부 내에서도 이러한 주장을 지지할 사람들이 분명히 있을 것입니다. 하지만 제 우려는 트럼프가 문제를 다루는 방식이 다르다는 점입니다. 가장 우려되는 점은, 그가 '적들과 어떻게 대처할 것인가?'라는 질문에 대해 '나는 동맹국이 필요 없다. 내가 직접 적들과 교섭할 것이다'라는 대답을 했다는 점입니다. 그는 시진핑, 푸틴, 김정은과 같은 인물들에게 매력을 느끼는 경향이 있습니다.

트럼프의 직접 교섭이 정말 좋은 거래로 이어져 안정과 평화가 이루어진다면 괜찮을 수는 있겠지만, 만약 그가 해결되지 않은 문제들에 대해 단기적이고 쉬운 거래를 추구한다면, 이는 매우 심각한 우려를 불러일으킬 것입니다. 그래서 저는 트럼프 2기에 대해 매우 솔직하고 정직한 우려를 표명하고자 합니다. 저는 트럼프의 가장 부정적인 경향들이 2기 행정부에서 더욱 두드러질 것이라고 생각합니다. 트럼프 1기 행정부에서는 많은 사람들이 그 경향들을 완화하려고 노력했지만, 2기 행정부에서는 그 경향들이 더욱 강화될 가능성이 크다고 우려하고 있습니다.

전광우 이사장: 차 박사님 답변 감사합니다. 필립 회장님, 매우 깊이 있는 내용의 의견과 질문을 주셔서 감사합니다. 시간이 다 되어가지만, 마치기전에 마지막으로 몇 가지 질문을 드리도록 하겠습니다.

먼저 외교 문제 관련 전문가이신 서울대학교 김병연 교수님께서 "트럼프와 김정은과의 조기 협상에 찬성하는 이유와 반대하는 이유에 대한 논의는 매우 흥미롭고 중요한 문제이지만, 트럼프 2기 행정부가 김정은과의 대화에 앞서 김정은과 푸틴을 분리하는 방법에 대해 고민하거나, 그렇게 해야 한다고 생각할 가능성이 있는지 궁금합니다"라는 질문을 주셨습니다. 어떻게 보시는지요?

빅터 차 박사: 질문 감사합니다. 개인적인 의견으로는, 조기 협상에 유리한 요인들과 반대로 이를 저지할 수 있는 요인들 중에서 가장 중요한 것은 아마도 북한이 미국과 대화할 필요가 없다는 점이라고 생각합니다.

현재 북한과 러시아의 관계가 매우 강하게 형성되어 있기 때문에, 김정은은 다시 한 번 트럼프와 만나 또 다른 실패가 될 수도 있는 회담을 할 이유가 없습니다. 여러 면에서 현재로서는 그런 대화를 시도할 필요를 느끼지 않는다고 봅니다. 지금 북한과 러시아를 분리하는 것은 매우 어렵다고 생각합니다. 북한은 중국으로부터 원하는 모든 것을 얻었고, 이제는 러시아로부터도 그에 상응하는 것을 얻고 있습니다. 이렇게 되면 북한과 러시아를 분리하는 것은 더욱 어려워집니다.

제가 생각하는 유일한 방법은 우크라이나 전쟁이 종료되는 경우입니다. 만약 우크라이나 전쟁이 끝난다면, 러시아는 더 이상 북한 군의 지원을 필요로 하지 않게 될 것입니다. 러시아는 당장 북한의 탄약을 그리 절실히 필요로 하지 않게 되며, 사실 탄약에 대한 관계는 장기적인 거래일 수는 있지만, 당장은 그다지 긴급한 상황이 아닙니다. 그리고 더 많은 북한 군인들이 사망하거나 포로로 잡히는 상황이 벌어지면, 이는 김정은에게 매우 큰 수치가 될 수 있으며, 그가 추가 병력을 파병하는 데에 부담이 될 것입니다.

따라서 아이러니하게도, 미국이 북한을 직접적으로 러시아와 분리하는 데에는 그리 많은 영향을 미칠 수 없다고 생각합니다. 이 문제를 해결할 수 있는 가장 효과적인 방법은 오히려 러시아의 북한 지원에 대한 필요를 줄이는 것이라고 봅니다.

전광우 이사장: 감사합니다. 이제 마지막으로 한 가지 질문을 드리겠습니다. 저는 현재 한국 정치에서 일어나고 있는 혼란의 결과가 어떻든 간에, 한미일 삼국의 동맹은 앞으로도 반드시 지지되고 강화되어야 한다고 생각합니다. 이는 우리 나라의 미래와 동북아시아의 평화를 위해서도 매우 중요한 일이라고 봅니다. 이와 관련해, 우리가 직면한 지정학적 도전에 대응하는 데 있어 한미일 삼국 동맹이 앞으로 어떤 역할을 할 것이라고 보시는지 말씀해 주실 수 있을까요? 새로운 트럼프 행정부와 동북아시아에 어떠한 메시지를 주실 수 있을 까요?

빅터 차 박사: 한미일 삼국 간 관계는 정말 중요하다고 생각합니다. 이는 매우 중요한 사안입니다. 그리고 트럼프 행정부에 전하고자 하는 요점은 삼국동맹 자체가 바로 그들의 아이디어였다는 점입니다. 즉, 삼국 간 협력에 처음으로 집중한 주체가 바로 그들이었습니다. 물론 바이든 행정부가 이를 훨씬 더 확장했지

만, 처음으로 삼국주의에 초점을 맞춘 것은 트럼프 행정부였습니다. 그래서 저는 그들이 이 방향을 계속해서 추진할 것이라 믿습니다. 트럼프 행정부 인수위원회 담당자들과 이야기를 나눠본 결과, 그들은 삼국 간 관계와 지금까지 이루어진 성과에 대해 매우 긍정적으로 평가하고 있습니다. 일본 정부 역시 이를 적극적으로 지지하고 있습니다.

결국 중요한 점은 한국 정부에 달려 있습니다. 다음 정권이 삼국 간 협력에 지속적으로 집중할 것인지가 핵심입니다. 윤 대통령이 일본과의 관계 및 삼국동맹에 대한 새로운 서사를 창출한 것은 매우 용기 있는 결정이었다고 봅니다. 이는 전 세계적으로 큰 인정을 받았습니다. 물론 한국 국내 정치에서는 그만큼 주목받지 않았을 수 있지만, 세계적으로는 매우 큰 인정을 받았습니다.

전광우 이사장: 잘 알겠습니다. 감사합니다. 바쁜 일정에 오늘 저희와 함께해 주셔서 감사합니다. 건승을 기원합니다.

빅터 차 박사: 네. 다음에는 직접 뵙기를 고대합니다. 감사합니다.

Korea's Political and Security Crisis: U.S.-ROK Alliance and North Korea Strategy under Trump 2.0

Victor Cha

Victor Cha

Dr. Cha is currently a Distinguished University Professor at Georgetown University. He is also President of the Geopolitics and Foreign and Korea Chair at CSIS, the Center for Strategic and International Studies. Dr. Cha is former Director for Asian Affairs at the White House National Security Council, and has served as President George W. Bush's top advisor on North Korean affairs. He holds a PhD in political science from Columbia University.

[Jan. 17, 2025]

Korea's Political and Security Crisis: U.S.-ROK Alliance and North Korea Strategy under Trump 2.0

Victor Cha
Distinguished University Professor, Georgetown University
President, Geopolitics and Foreign Policy Department and
Korea Chair, CSIS

Jun Kwang-woo: Good morning, ladies and gentlemen. Welcome to the IGE Forum.

Today, we are most fortunate to have an outstanding guest speaker, Dr. Victor Cha, a leading international authority on US foreign policy, especially regarding Northeast Asia. He will be joining us live from Hawaii while traveling to discuss key diplomatic and security issues in the face of rising geopolitical challenges, including US-China tensions, North Korea's provocations, and the deepening alliance between North Korea and Russia. We expect that he will explore strategic implications for South Korea, particularly in the context of Trump 2.0 and the recent political turmoil in Korea.

Dr. Cha is currently a Distinguished University Professor at Georgetown University, and also President of the Geopolitics and Foreign Policy Department and Korea Chair at CSIS (the Center for Strategic and International Studies). Dr. Cha is former Director for Asian Affairs for the White House's National Security Council, and has served as President George W. Bush's top advisor on North Korean affairs. He holds a PhD in Political Science from Columbia University and in 2023, was named the Distinguished University Professor, the highest honor bestowed upon a tenured faculty at Georgetown University.

Without further ado, let's welcome Dr. Victor Cha who will speak first for about 30 minutes, followed by the discussion and Q&A as scheduled. Dr. Cha, floor is yours.

Victor Cha: Thank you very much, Dr. Jun. It's very good to be with you again in the IGE seminar.

Today, I'm going to focus my initial remarks on seven broad points on South Korea, on Trump and the US-Korea alliance, and on North Korea, that I thought about for the seminar. I think that will give us enough of a basis for discussion.

The first point, which is obvious to everyone, is the prolonged domestic political instability and leadership vacuum in South Korea that really has the ability to impact everything and all the issues that we're talking about.

In general, I think most have analyzed this, both on the economic and the political side, as unfortunate. But at the same time, I think there is a hope that the impact will be minimalized. After all, what is happening now in Korea is not the first time. We know that in recent history, it's happened at least two other times in 2004 and 2016, both with different outcomes. But in the end, the main message for many government institutions, academics, experts, is that in the previous cases, we saw eventually the politics recovered, the economics recovered, and certainly everyone hopes that that is the case this time around.

I will say that I do have some concern on the economic side that a protracted crisis, something that is not resolved along the timeline that most people are talking about, which is the early to mid-summer, if it's not all resolved at that point, there could be broader and longer-term repercussions.

The reason I say that is because if we look at the explanations for why there was minimal damage after the 2004 impeachment and the 2016 impeachment, they point to factors or causal variables that I would argue were present in 2004 and in 2016, but are arguably not present in 2025. In the case of 2004, the overturned impeachment of Roh Moo-Hyun, this did have an initial economic and political impact on the country. But in the end, economic gains were recouped, and the politics resumed and the Roh Moo-Hyun administration finished their time in office. But one of the big factors there that contributed to a quick and early recovery for South Korea from the political crisis was the fact that we were seeing double-digit Chinese economic growth. That was a variable.

Chinese economic growth was a variable that was helping the Korean economy to recover fairly quickly. It was also just after China had entered the WTO, the World Trade Organization. There was a lot happening on the economic side that helped with the Korean recovery.

In 2016-2017, when President Park Geun-hye was impeached and the Constitutional Court upheld the impeachment decision, there was also an economic impact. But the economic impact was somewhat minimized by what at the time was really quite successful, quite positive growth in the export sector for semiconductors, the semiconductor industry. That was a huge boon to the Korean economy that allowed for there to be minimal economic damage despite the political crisis that had occurred.

The point I'm making here is that if we look at 2025 and a protracted crisis, neither of those two economic variables are arguably there. China is not growing like it was in 2004. The semiconductor export sector, while it's still healthy, was certainly not at the levels it was in 2016 and 2017.

In addition to that, and not at all insignificant, we're still certainly in the middle of one war in Europe and possibly out of another war in the Middle East. In addition to that, we have uncertainty with regard to the incoming Trump administration and what sort of economic actions he might take against allies. The point here is that if this crisis goes beyond the summer, again, many of the variables that contributed to sort of fairly rapid economic recovery, political recovery, are arguably not there in 2025 like they were in 2004 and 2016.

A protracted crisis also puts South Korea in a bad situation regarding its dealings with the incoming Trump administration. Right now, the only prominent figure who has met with Trump and Elon Musk on the Korean side has been from the private sector, a CEO of Shinsegae Group who had visited Mar-a-Lago at the invitation of Donald Trump Jr. That CEO, as well as the CEO of another economic group in South Korea, are the only ones that are being invited to attend Trump's inauguration. The concerns here that are emerging is that a South Korean government, which is in a state of diplomatic standstill due to the leadership vacuum, will face some difficulties in responding to President-elect Trump once he starts office.

I'm going to talk about that more in a minute in a little bit more detail. The second larger point is that North Korea remains a persistent security risk, but this persistent security risk could be also exacerbated by the prolonged domestic political instability. Under the Biden administration, we have seen a total of 162 North Korean provocations, including 90 missile launching events and 32 waves of balloon launches.

This is the most ever under any US administration since 1953. During the first Trump administration, there were a total of 41 provocations, including 35 missile demonstrations, one nuclear test, and five other types of provocations. The Trump administration and South Korean administration are dealing with a much more belligerent and somewhat unrestrained North Korea.

The concern is about some sort of miscalculation by Kim Jong-un. South Korea's domestic crisis, North Korea was first a bit cautious to respond to the instability. But as the situation goes longer and longer, North Korea may also find this favorable to some sort of provocative actions.

As we all know, they recently tested an IRBM on January 6th, claiming it to be a hypersonic missile. This was the first test of 2025, right before Trump's inauguration, and the first since the short-range ballistic missile launch on November 4th in 2024, around the time of the US election. North Korea may be primed for some sort of miscalculation because they like to do belligerent acts at the start of a new US administration. So, they see the start of the Trump administration as an opportunity where they might do that. At the start of the Obama administration, they did a nuclear test. At the start of the last Trump administration, they also did a thermonuclear test.

The one exception to this rule was the first year of the Biden administration, where North Korea did not do anything. But that I think is attributable to the fact that they were in COVID lockdown at that time, which probably stopped them from doing anything. But they certainly made up for that last year by all the actions they've taken over the past couple of years.

And then, of course, the strengthened Russian-DPRK relationship dangerously may provide North Korea with new missile technologies that they will want to demonstrate. New missile technology, perhaps new submarine technologies that they may want to demonstrate. Plus, this new security treaty between the two sides may make North Korea feel overconfident.

At the same time, though, North Korea could be more cautious because if they carry out provocations that might give legitimacy to Yun's martial law, as the declaration stated and talked about anti-state pro-North Korean activities, an unnecessary escalation might be counterproductive as North Korea has sent troops to support Russia while also taking defensive measures like destroying roads and inter-Korean connections along the border.

That's the second major point. The third major point is with regard to the Trump administration. And here, one of the main concerns is how Trump will respond to the special measures agreement and defense cost sharing issue. The current SMA agreement, which is the 12th SMA agreement, covers from 2026 to 2030. The United States and South Korea set the first year, 2026, of defense cost sharing at a little over $1 billion, which is an 8.3% increase from 2025. And as you are well aware, the Biden administration proposed renewing the SMA prematurely, early, even though it had two more years left on it as a preemptive action to try to avert alliance tensions and a lack of agreement, as we saw during the first Trump administration.

But now with Trump coming into office, there are concerns that he could tear up or withdraw from the agreement or pressure South Korea to renegotiate the agreement. And my guess is that when this was renegotiated between the US and South Korea, it really wasn't something that Trump had any attention to because he was focused on the campaign. But as some of you may have read, when he was asked about it in a press interview, he said that South Korea should pay $10 billion a year for cost sharing. He said this in October.

And the fourth, I think, concern is with regard to troop withdrawal. Trump views many allies as freeloading on security while the US is in a trade deficit with US troops hosted by allies.

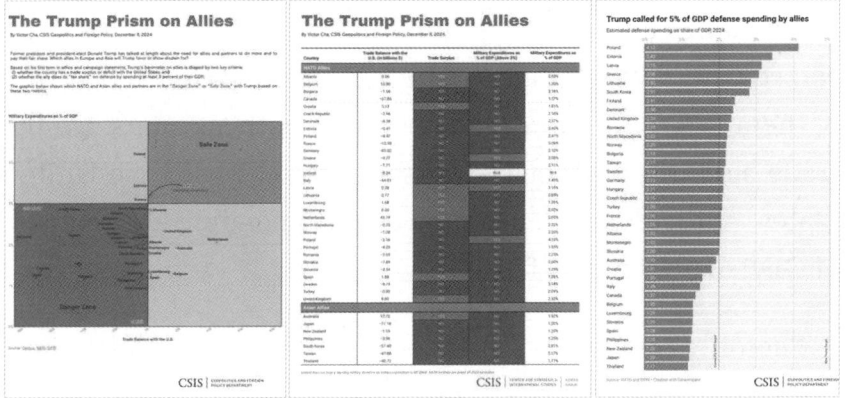

Okay. So this was a slide we put together that pretty much, I think, sums up how Trump views allies and partners. He views them basically along two axes.

One of them has to do with trade, merchandise trade, and whether an ally or partner has a trade surplus or deficit with the United States. And the second axis is in terms of defense spending and whether the country or the partner or the ally is spending enough. And we defined enough as 3% of GDP on national defense.

And we picked these two axes because this is basically the way Trump has always talked about allies and partners, that they're cheating him on trade, and that the US is paying for everyone's defense and that they're free riding off US defense commitments. He said this during his first term in office. He continues to say it now. And it's been something he's believed going back for decades.

So what we did was we plotted all NATO allies and Indo-Pacific allies and partners along these two axes. And as you can see, every NATO ally and Indo-Pacific partner, or many of them in Trump's eyes, fail on one or both accounts. On the trade side, they either run a trade surplus with the United States. And on the defense side, they're spending less than 3% of GDP on national defense.

The only NATO ally that meets Trump's criteria is, and I think you can barely see it on the screen there, the only one that meets Trump's criteria is Latvia. And the only Indo-Pacific ally that does not completely fail from Trump's perspective is Australia. Australia is the only Indo-Pacific ally that runs a trade deficit with the United States. All other allies run a trade surplus, including South Korea's, which is on the order of $51.4 billion, which is the fourth highest trade surplus with the United States behind Germany, Japan, and Canada among NATO and US allies.

South Korea has had concerns in the past over Trump talking about withdrawing forces from South Korea. On the one hand, some of these fears were ameliorated because there was bipartisan agreement in the US Congress during Trump's first term in office on the necessity of maintaining US forces in Korea.

As long as that bipartisan support was there, that was a pretty stable position for things to be in. But today, as Trump enters office, it's not necessarily true that that bipartisan consensus exists. Moreover, and perhaps most importantly, the 2025 National Defense Authorization Act, which used to have a clause in it that limited the ability of the US administration to withdraw forces from Korea, it limited their ability to do that. That was in the National Defense Authorization Act during Trump's time in office. Today, it is no longer in the National Defense Authorization Act. Congress's check on Trump's ability to take actions like pull troops from Korea or from Germany, that check is no longer there. In large part, because during the four years of the Biden administration, there was no need for it. Biden was not going to pull troops from Korea or Germany. But I think it's certainly a concern now.

The fourth point I wanted to mention has to do with concerns about tariffs. As I said, Trump looks at a country like Korea and sees massive trade surpluses and also sees defense spending lower. Again, we said 3%. Apparently, at some point, he was asked about this and he said 3% was not enough. It had to be 5%, in which case no country, no Indo-Pacific or NATO ally meets that number.

But there is a concern that Trump is considering declaring a national economic emergency to permit a new tariff program. This sort of declaration would allow Trump to construct a new tariff program using something called the International Economic Emergency Powers Act or IEEPA, which unilaterally authorizes the president to manage imports during a national emergency. This has certainly raised concerns in South Korea. It partly is one of the reasons why we've seen further depreciation of the Korean currency.

Of course, it's not the only reason. But this is a real concern that we could see either 10% across-the-board tariffs, new types of tariff schemes through IEPA, and then also something that I think we're starting to see already, which is another provision in the Trade Act that allows the United States not to do across-the-board tariffs, but to target certain companies and impose import quotas on certain companies. I think that would more likely be applied to places like companies in China, but those are the other sorts of things.

The fifth point is with regard to what could happen between a Trump administration and North Korea. There are some subsets here, but let me just put them into three categories. The first is concerns that the United States might move more to an arms control paradigm with North Korea and dispense with CVID, complete, verifiable, and irreversible denuclearization.

There was a report in December of 2023 that Trump was considering a plan to let North Korea keep its nuclear weapons and offer the regime financial incentives to stop them from vertically proliferating, that is making more nuclear weapons or more long-range ICBMs, but entering some sort of arms control negotiations where they would keep their weapons, but they would stop making ones that were most threatening to the United States. This would be very concerning for South Korea, but I think Trump is well aware that the previous attempts at negotiation failed when it came to denuclearization. Some have said that this is something that they might be considering. That is point five.

Point six is there are concerns about decoupling. Trump might not rule out the possibility of offering partial sanctions relief to North Korea, again, on the conditions that they stop development of those capabilities that threaten the U.S. homeland, but not necessarily focusing on those capabilities that threaten the Korean Peninsula. Both this and an arms control deal would be a form of decoupling in the alliance because it would mean that the United States was negotiating for only its own security and not the security of allies. It would also have the effect of legitimizing North Korea's status as a de facto nuclear weapon state, which is, of course, a big concern for South Korea.

I've lost track of my points, but related to this is the concern about what's called Korea passing in the US – DPRK negotiation talks, especially if there is no functioning government in South Korea six months or longer into a Trump administration. If there's no functioning government in South Korea, then the chance of Korea passing becomes very, very high. Of course, the acting government is doing the best it can today to maintain regular contact with the Biden administration. Foreign Minister Cho has been very active.

The National Security Advisor has been very active. Vice Ministers in the Ministry of Foreign Affairs have been very active. The Defense Minister has been very active.

But, you know, everybody in the U.S., and particularly in a new Trump administration, knows that this is not the government they're going to be dealing with. They're going to be dealing with a new government. And I hope it's not the case, but I think it will be harder. I mean, a Biden administration was very receptive to continuing to do lots of meetings with the South Korean side to ensure that there was continuity. I'm worried that a Trump administration will not be as interested in doing these meetings until a new government is in place.

And then the sixth point is the concern about a potential, in quotation marks, early deal with North Korea. And particularly if we see more and more North Korean provocations, there may be pressure on Trump to try to deal with this issue sooner rather than later. Obviously, he'll be very focused on domestic issues, like tax cuts, like the border, immigration. And then internationally, the focus will be on trying to cement this peace in Gaza, as well as the war in Ukraine.

But he may also be thinking about an early deal with North Korea for three reasons. The first is that Trump is a very confident individual, and he has met and has maintained contact with Kim Jong-un for quite some time. And so, he might feel like he has a great deal of confidence in dealing with North Korea, and that might contribute to him engaging early on.

Second possible favorable factor for an early deal is the absence of high-level officials who would restrain Trump. During his first term, you had people like H.R. McMaster, John Bolton, two of his national security advisors, Secretary Jim Mattis, all who tried to restrain Trump from doing things that might be too risky or too dangerous. I think we're seeing with the appointments in the second term under Trump is that the primary criteria for these people is not whether they pass muster with the mainstream Republican establishment.

The main criteria is whether they are 100% loyal to Trump. So, I think in particular, we see this in the appointments, the potential appointments at Secretary of Defense and Director of National Intelligence, where he's clearly appointing Attorney General, where he's clearly appointing people who are extremely loyal to Trump. So the internal restraints might not be there.

Then the third reason for a possible early deal is working in the opposite fashion, in the sense that he might seek an early deal with North Korea as a way to gain leverage over the alliance with South Korea in advance of a new government coming in. In other words, he might seek an early deal with North Korea to have better leverage in terms of SMA renegotiations or to have better leverage in terms of talking about troop withdrawals or peace treaty with North Korea, these sorts of things. So all of these are quite different and paradigm shifting scenarios.

My final and seventh point is that while these are things that we really need to think about and be concerned about with regard to a second Trump administration, there still are some restraining factors that might cause him not to go so immediately to some sort of early deal.

The first of these, as I already mentioned, is that he may not simply may not be able to have the time or the bandwidth to prioritize North Korea, given all of the other issues that he's very focused on seeing early action on. Again, the war in Ukraine, tariffs, the war in Gaza, the border, immigration issues. It wouldn't surprise me if a lot of the initial executive orders are focused on those sorts of things, rather than focusing on the negotiation with North Korea. The negotiation with North Korea would take a lot of time and energy. It would take a lot of his personal time and energy, and he just may not have time for that immediately.

Second potential restraining factor from some sort of early deal is the opposite of what I said earlier, is that Trump may have confidence in his ability to talk to Kim Jong-un and to negotiate with him, but he also may not trust Kim Jong-un based on the failure of the Hanoi summit and based on the fact that he thought they had an agreement in the Singapore summit and then the failure after the Hanoi summit, and then the absence of any further progress after the meeting in Panmunjom.

If the first reason that we might not see an immediate deal with North Korea is that they'll be focused on Ukraine, tariffs, Gaza, the border, immigration. The second is that he may not just trust that Kim is able to make the sort of deal that he wants. Then the third reason we might not see an early deal has less to do with the United States and has more to do with DPRK and Russia. This relationship has become extremely strong. It's a renewal of the Cold War era type security guarantee and alliance that the two countries shared during the Cold War. There's a great deal that North Korea is now getting from Russia in terms of food and fuel and medicine and all sorts of things that simply might make it less. North Korea may have less of an incentive to deal with the United States because of this very big and growing relationship with Russia. They may just not see the need for that.

In 2017-2018, North Korea was in a different position. It didn't have a strong relationship with Russia, didn't have a strong relationship with China, and maybe they saw a need to do that. But in North Korea's current situation with a very strong relationship with Russia, increasing efforts by China to get closer to North Korea as a result of the relationship with Russia, the North Koreans may feel no need at all to deal with Trump, at least for the time being. This would be the third possible reason that there might be restraint from an early deal.

There's plenty to think about here as we approach the inauguration of the new US president, as we sit and watch what is happening in South Korea's own domestic politics.

From my perspective in Washington DC, all the questions that I get these days really don't have anything to do with North Korea or anything to do with what the Trump administration is going to do. All the questions really have to do with what's going on in South Korea these days and how soon or how long it will take for the political crisis to be resolved. Given the broader context in the world today and the role that Yoon was playing in terms of really stepping up South Korea's global presence, participating in the G7, participating in NATO, providing support in Ukraine, at a very key moment where many global governance and liberal-based institutions are under stress, regardless of what has been happening domestically for Yoon, they saw what Yoon was doing on the global stage as very important. I've heard this in Japan, in Southeast Asia, all over Europe. There was a lot of approval for what Korea's 12th or 13th largest economy in the world was doing, stepping up on both the political and on the economic side.

Because of that, there's a great deal of attention right now on what's happening in South Korea, and I hope that it will all be resolved in the not-too-distant future.

Dr. Jun, with that, I think I've gone over my time limit. Thank you very much, everyone, for listening. I'm looking forward to our discussion.

Jun Kwang-woo: Thank you very much, Victor, for your brilliant opening speech, which covered a comprehensive picture of the stakes we have at this very critical moment, with the new administration coming on board starting next week, Trump 2.0, whereas Korea's internal domestic political environment, as you described, is very precarious. It's a very disturbing situation. But as you pointed out, Korea has a long track record to rebound from a very tough, challenging environment crisis, whether that is economic or political, in the past. So, we are very much hoping to demonstrate again our exceptional resilience in coping with this impending turmoil we are now facing.

Now, let me move on to the follow-up discussion and Q&A session. Today we invited three distinguished discussants. First, we have invited Chairman Ki-hak Sung, who you know quite well, to join us as a commentator or say hi to you. Also, Ambassador Ahn Ho-young, a former Korean ambassador to the United States. Also, we invited a foreign speaker, who is the chairperson of the European Chamber of Commerce in Korea, because I thought it would be useful to hear some foreign perspective of the situation over here and in the Northeast Asia. So I invited him to join us later as well.

Now, we have a great privilege to invite Mr. Ki-hak Sung, Chairman of Youngone Trading Group. He is traveling now and today in Vietnam. As you know well, Chairman Sung is widely respected for his distinguished entrepreneurial leadership as well as generous support for philanthropic activities around the world. Let's welcome Chairman Sung.

Ki-hak Sung: Dr. Cha, it is a great pleasure to attend this gathering, and I sincerely appreciate your detailed explanation of the current situation.

At the moment, I am more concerned about domestic issues in Korea rather than external matters. Recently, there has been a shift in the political landscape, and discussions regarding the government's policies are becoming increasingly active among the public. As a result, there seems to be growing attention on these topics. Notably, the popularity of the ruling party and the current leadership has risen sharply. This is the situation I am observing domestically.

However, I have noticed that the pressure from North Korea seems to have lessened compared to before. While there is a possibility that the strengthening of the alliance between Russia and North Korea could lead to technical support that may enhance North Korea's military capabilities, outside of that, I feel that the pressure from North Korea has reduced considerably.

That said, China continues to exert significant influence, which remains a key issue we must closely monitor. From an economic perspective, China's oversupply is severely impacting industries in Korea and neighboring countries. As a result, many industries are collapsing, and it is crucial for us to carefully examine this situation and explore ways to protect our domestic industries.

Unfortunately, at such a critical time, the increasing political uncertainty in Korea could have a significant impact on the public's trust in the government.

Dr. Cha, once again, I would like to express my gratitude for your insightful presentation today. There are many aspects I would like to discuss further, and should the opportunity arise, I look forward to meeting with you in person to gain a deeper understanding of the current situation. Thank you very much.

Jun Kwang-woo: Thank you very much. Next, we have Ambassador Ahn. He has also served as Vice Minister of Foreign Affairs and International Trade, among many other prominent positions. Ambassador Ahn, welcome.

Ahn Ho-young: Victor, let me start by thanking you for taking time to speak to us in the middle of your very hectic schedule. Thank you again for your seven points. I wish to make common-sounding questions on your point five and six.

Your point five was on the possibility of the Trump administration moving the objective of gold for North Korean nuclear issues from denuclearization to arms control. And your sixth point was the possibility of decoupling strategic interests of the United States and Korea along the way. So, when I was listening to those five and six points, then two questions came up in my mind, which is that how in fact high is the possibility of that taking place?

Because you know it, I know it, North Korean nuclear issue is under heavy review by the transition committee, in my mind, which is going to take some more time. So, how do you think high the likelihood of that in fact happening in the Trump administration?

The second question in my mind was, well, were it to happen, that is to say, moving the objective from denuclearization to arms control and decoupling strategic interests between Korea and then the United States?

Again, I don't have to explain to you what impact it will have upon Korea. It in fact would create a wholly different geo-strategic and geo-political and even geo-economic condition for Korea. And then, well, Chairman Sung, he just mentioned China.

And then the way I look upon it is that China seems to be, in a sense, seeing a certain positive side when Mr. Trump is coming back to power, in the sense that because there is a high likelihood that the alliance relationship between the United States and the other allies of the United States, it in fact could be alienated. And then that in fact would create an opportunity for China. That's there.

And then that in fact is something which could happen in case of change of Trump administration's focus from denuclearization to arms control, et cetera, et cetera. And then at the same time, again, I don't have to explain to you that there will be very heavy pressure in South Korea that we must develop our own nuclear weapons. So all those questions came up in my mind.

My second point is about restraining factors. And then you just shared with us about three restraining factors. And I was wondering, as additional restraining factors, I was thinking about at least two restraining factors.

One, the role of the Congress. And then recently the chairperson for the Senate Armed Services Committee Mr. Wicker and Senate Foreign Relations Committee Mr. Risch were appointed. And again, Victor, I don't have to explain to you what they think about the allies, what they think about Korea, and then what they think about North Korean nuclear issue.

And I'm pretty sure even in the House, the leadership in the House for Arms Control Committee and then Foreign Affairs Committee could in fact be the leaders of the same mold. So that in fact was one restraining factor during Trump one. And I was wondering if it could be, continue to be, a restraining factor under Trump two as well.

And then another restraining factor, which came up in my mind is Victor Cha. Of course, you could in fact, put senses into those people who are working on North Korean dossier in the Trump administration.

If I could make one additional point, I was just listening to you. And I was reminded about early days of Trump administration back in 2017. And that was reminded in February, Mr. Mattis came to visit Korea. In March, Mr. Tillerson came to visit Korea. And in April, Mr. Pence, the vice president came to visit Korea. And then of course, at the time, Mr. Hwang Kyo-ahn was an acting president. But at the same time, those leaders came to visit Korea, even if they were having very busy time during the early days of the inauguration. So I really appreciated it. But at the same time, I think there was a very firm intention on the part of Trump administration to show to the Koreans that we, I mean, United States is firmly committed to the alliance between Korea and the United States. So let me stop there. Thank you once again.

Victor Cha: Thank you. Thank you for all of these wonderful comments from both Chairman Sung and Ambassador Ahn. It's only in the IGE seminar that when someone gives a presentation, they get comments from a

CEO chairman of a business and an ambassador. It shows the high level of group that Dr. Jun brings together. I know we're short on time, so I will try to answer these as concisely as I can.

First, I think it's very interesting, Chairman Sung, that you said that you saw the Russian prime minister is in Vietnam at this particular time. This is not well reported around the world, but there clearly is a strategy that Putin is following with regard to Vietnam. Of course, when he went to Pyongyang, he also went to Vietnam. I think he really sees these two pieces—North Korea and Vietnam—as a very important part of China's reestablishment of its position in Asia, and in particular in ways that are very disconcerting to, at the same time, both the United States and China.

If he were to pick two countries where he thought he could make the most inroads in ways that would dislodge the traditional positions of the United States and China in the region, it's these two countries. I think this is part of a real effort.

On the recent popularity of the PPP, I've read that they're now up to 40 points and within the margin of error with the DP, which is something I think that many Americans did not expect. I do not know what that means for the fate of President Yoon, but I think from a U.S. perspective, it is an important sign that the Korean public, even though they may have differing views about what President Yoon did on

December 3, is interpreted in the U.S. as meaning the Korean public certainly liked the foreign policies of the PPP and President Yoon. I think that's a very important message to send.

On the whole question of decoupling and the deal with North Korea, I think about it in terms of is Trump more inclined to try to get an easy deal or try to get a hard deal?

A hard deal is CVID when you're talking about nuclear weapons, long-range ballistic missiles, and short-range ballistic missiles. That's a hard deal. An easy deal is one in which you just stop nuclear testing and stop missile testing, long-range missile testing, and you don't worry about the other sorts of things.

I think Trump is much more inclined to the easy deal. He's much more inclined to the easy deal. He said in his first term when Shinzo Abe and others talked about short-range testing, he said he doesn't care about short-range missiles. Everybody has them, I think was his quote. That's not a good sign.

With regard to China, I think absolutely China sees real opportunities to make inroads in a Trump administration, even though I think they were very concerned about how much progress the Biden administration made in terms of the bilateral alliances. Camp David, AUKUS, IPEF, the Quad made real progress there. I think they think that they can undo a lot of that under Trump because Trump won't care about that as much.

In terms of Congress and others like other people who could try to restrain Trump, I think those people are there. I think there are people in Congress that would not want to withdraw troops. I think people like Alex Wong as Deputy National Security Advisor, Ivan Kanapathy as Senior Director for NSC, all of these people are in the right place when it comes to foreign policy to the region. The problem is they're not going to be making the policy. Trump's going to be dictating the policy, and they're just going to be trying to catch up.

Finally, on the early visits by Tillerson and Pence to Korea in 2017 and 2018, meeting with acting president, I feel like that situation was different in two ways.

The first is these early visits by Tillerson and others were in part the result of internal competition in the Trump administration, where they were trying to fight over who should control foreign policy. We see it in McMaster's book. McMaster and Tillerson had fierce arguments about this. I think that was part of it.

The other part of it was there was a desire to show strong ties with South Korea because North Korea was doing all of these things, and Trump really didn't know how to handle North Korea. He did not know what to do at that point. For those reasons, both the internal bureaucratic fight as well as not knowing what to do with North Korea, so the best thing was to be with the ally, that's what led to the early visits. But this time around, Trump knows how to deal with North Korea. He's not worried about that. There won't be an internal bureaucratic battle over who controls the policy because Trump controls the policy. For this reason, I'm more worried about Korea passing, what I mentioned earlier about Korea passing.

Jun Kwang-woo: Thank you for your brilliant feedback. Next, last but not least, commentator, Mr. Philippe Van Hoof. He is the chairperson of the European Chamber of Commerce here in Korea. Also, he is the country head, and country manager of ING Bank in Korea as well. Philippe, welcome to our forum today.

Philippe Van Hoof: Thank you so much, Chairman Jun. I also want to express my sincere gratitude to Distinguished Professor Cha, Chairman Sung, and Ambassador Ahn. I will try not to repeat the excellent points they've made, but instead expand on a couple of things, particularly based on Professor Cha's remarks.

First, I fully align with your observation regarding your numerous trips to Brussels and your recognition that Europe has now become more aware of the link to APEC. I can personally confirm that from my own experience. Meeting with Ambassador Ryu, the Korean Ambassador to the

European Union, last October was a pivotal moment for me. Walking through the halls of the European Commission, it was evident that Europe understands that global stability is unattainable without stability in both the North Atlantic and the North Pacific. This aligns closely with the remarks made by a former Japanese Prime Minister. Additionally, Japan's invitation to the upcoming NATO Summit in Madrid this June carries significant weight and is certainly an important development. So, I can confidently say that Europe fully acknowledges the importance of stability in the North Pacific.

Secondly, I'd like to share a brief comment about our recent engagements. In the past month, we've had the privilege of meeting with key Korean leaders, including Acting President Choi, and Minister of Trade, Industry, and Energy Dukgeun Ahn. We also met with Mayor Oh of Seoul, the Governor of Gyeonggi Province, and the Chairman of the Financial Services Commission, among others. These kinds of opportunities are unparalleled. No other country offers such focused attention and engagement with foreign investors. This is true not only for our organization but also for AMCHAM and other major foreign chambers. The messages we've received have been incredibly strong. We have seen the resilience of Korea's democratic system, and we've observed that our members continue to operate business as usual, despite the challenges.

This is just a brief contribution from me, but I felt it was important to share with you because sometimes the media presents a different image of Korea. I have repeatedly emphasized to Acting President Choi that the reports submitted by foreign subsidiaries—particularly those from European companies—are actually of greater importance than many realize. These "business-as-usual" reports play a critical role in understanding the actual business environment and are vital to foreign investors' trust and confidence.

Now, to shift to a question I'd like to pose. I've heard all of the concerns regarding the relationship between Korea and the United States as a key ally. However, I'd like to approach this from a different perspective—if I may, without being too provocative. What would the United States look like without its allies? In my view, the U.S. is inherently a maritime power. It requires access to the North Atlantic, and today, above all, it needs access to the North Pacific. To ensure this, the U.S. requires strong allies across both the Atlantic and the Pacific. So, that's my very straightforward question.

Victor Cha: Thank you, Mr. Van Hoof, for these comments and the question. I think I've made more trips to Brussels in the last year than I have to Seoul and Tokyo, in large part, because there is a great deal of interest in Europe now with regard to political and security issues in the Indo-Pacific, because they see them as directly impacting politics, security, and economics in Europe. I think that's a very important sign that the two regions are having much more of a dialogue these days on political and security issues than I've ever seen in my 30 years studying these issues. So, I entirely agree with this phrase that you use, no stability in the North Atlantic unless there's stability in the North Pacific. I think that's an excellent phrase, and I think that really sums up the level of discussion and cooperation.

I will also say that every time I go to Brussels, I feel like the conversation taking place among Europeans about North Pacific security now rivals that of the conversations we have in Washington, D.C. That was not the case five years ago, but it's very much the case today. And then the people they have at NATO, for example, who are working on the North Pacific and working on Japan and Korea are excellent. The level of policy is people, and if you don't have good people, they have really good people working on this.

Second is it's very good to hear that the acting government is reaching out to you, to your European colleagues, to the American business community to say that things are business as usual. It's a very important message to send. At one point, CSIS was part of a group that hosted the Federation of Korean Industries who came to Washington, D.C. And at one point, the U.S. Chamber was thinking, because of what was happening in Korea, that they should postpone the trip. But contrary to that, many people said, no, no, it has to look like business as usual. And besides, the Korean businessmen want to hear from the U.S. side what it's going to be like under Trump, too, and the American businessmen want to hear from the Korean side about what's going on in Korea, and they want to be able to have conversations, those clear channels. It's very important. So, I entirely agree with the business as usual.

On your question about shouldn't the U.S. need and want allies, whether we're talking about in terms of export controls or strategic competition, Russia, Ukraine, China, North Korea, Iran, the United States needs allies and partners. I agree with that 100 percent. I entirely agree with that view. And I think that there are many who will staff the Trump administration that will also make the same arguments internally. But my concern is that Trump just thinks about things differently. And what is most concerning to me is that his response to the question about how do you deal with adversaries without allies is his response is, I don't need allies because I'm going to engage the adversaries myself, right? And so we know he has this attraction to people like Xi Jinping and Putin and Kim Jong-un.

That would be fine if you were cutting really good deals that lead to stability and peace. But if you're just looking for easy deals that don't really address all the questions, I think that's where the concerns become very, very acute. So I'm giving you my very frank and honest opinion about what I'm worried about when it comes to Trump 2, because I think many of his worst tendencies will be facilitated in a second

Trump administration when in many ways there are people who are trying to mitigate those worst tendencies in the first Trump administration.

Jun Kwang-woo: Thank you Philippe, for your very thoughtful comments and questions as well. And also thank you, Dr. Cha, for your great response. Time has run out, but, Dr. Cha, if you don't mind, I would like to explore final questions before we wrap up.

First, Professor Kim Byung-yeon from Seoul National University, very prominent scholar in foreign affairs issues, has raised a very interesting and important point. He inquired, 'The discussion on the reasons for and against early negotiations between Trump and Kim Jong-un is a highly engaging and crucial issue. However, I am curious if there is a possibility that the second Trump administration might consider how to separate Kim Jong-un from Putin before engaging in dialogue with Kim Jong-un, or whether they might think this should be a priority.' How do you view this? Any quick comment?

Victor Cha: Yeah, I mean, I think of the factors that I mentioned, I tried to enumerate the factors in an objective fashion. My own personal opinion is I think of all those factors that might push for an early deal versus ones that might pull back. The most important one, I think, really is the North Korean need not to talk to the United States.

The strength of the relationship with Russia right now makes it such that Kim Jong-un really doesn't have a compelling need to gamble and try to talk with Trump again to have another failed meeting. I think in many ways, he doesn't need that at this point, which also speaks to the question. It's very, very hard right now, I think, to try to separate North Korea and Russia.

North Korea is getting everything that it could have possibly wanted from China. It's now getting from Russia. I think it makes it very hard to separate them.

The only avenue I see for doing this is if somehow the war in Ukraine stops, because if the war in Ukraine stops, then Russia has no need for North Korean troops. Russia has less immediate need for ammunition. I mean, I think that ammunition relationship is a long-term relationship, frankly, but has less immediate need for ammunition. And if many more North Korean troops are dying and getting captured, that could be very embarrassing for Kim Jong-un, and that might be a disincentive for him to send more troops.

So ironically, I don't think there's much the United States can do directly to North Korea to separate them from Russia. I think the best wedge into this is actually reducing Russian need for North Korean support.

Jun Kwang-woo: Okay, thank you very much, indeed. Dr. Cha, one closing comment that I would expect from you is about the importance of trilateral alliance that we have established a few years ago. And I think whatever the outcome we have from the ongoing upheaval here in Korean politics, I think that has to be supported, maintained, and strengthened for the future of this country, and also for the peace of Northeast Asia.

In that respect, what would you say to the Trump administration or the countries here in Northeast Asia about the likely role of this trilateral alliance amongst US, Japan, and Korea in dealing with the geopolitical challenges we face these days and in the future?

Victor Cha: I think it's very important, the trilateral relationship, Chairman Jun, I think it's extremely important. And I think the best argument to be made to the Trump administration is that it was their idea. I mean, they were the ones who actually started focusing on trilateralism. Of course, the Biden administration took it much further, but they were the ones who focused on it. And so I'm hopeful that they will continue to. I've talked to people involved in the transition, the Trump administration, and they do think very positively about trilateral relations and what has been accomplished thus far. And the government in Japan, of course, is very supportive of it too.

So the real question, again, comes down to the South

Korean government, and whether the next South Korean government, whatever government that might be, will continue to focus on this trilateralism. It was a very brave move by President Yoon to recreate a new narrative for the relationship with Japan and trilateralism.

And that is something that was recognized all around the world. It may not have been as appreciated as much in South Korean domestic politics, but around the world, it was hugely recognized.

Jun Kwang-woo: Great. Victor, thank you very much for sharing your exceptionally informative and insightful views with us today. I wish you all the best. And take care of yourself during your very hectic traveling schedule. See you next time.

Victor Cha: Okay, next time, see you in person. Thank you. Happy New Year.

세계경제연구원 특별강연
간행물 목록

IGE Publications

Occasional Paper Series

1993

	Title	Author
93-01	Clintonomics and the New World Order: Implications for Korea-US Relations	C. Fred Bergsten
93-02	The Uruguay Round, NAFTA and US-Korea Economic Relations	Jeffrey Schott

1994

	Title	Author
94-01	Korea in the World: Today and Tomorrow	Paul Kennedy
94-02	US-Japan Technological Competition and Implications for Korea	Ronald A. Morse
94-03	The Problems of the Japanese Economy and their Implications for Korea	Toyoo Gyohten
94-04	Changing US and World Economies and their Market Prospects	Allen Sinai
94-05	Prospects for New World Monetary System and Implications for Korea	John Williamson
94-06	The Promises of the WTO for the Trading Community	Arthur Dunkel

1995

	Title	Author
95-01	Mexican Peso Crisis and its Implications for the Global Financial Market	Charles H. Dallara
95-02	The World Economic Trend and US Economic Outlook	Allen Sinai
95-03	New Games, New Rules, and New Strategies	Lester Thurow
95-04	The United States and North Korea Future Prospects	Robert Scalapino
95-05	US Foreign Policy toward East Asia and the Korean Peninsula	James A. Baker III
95-06	US Trade Tension with Japan and their Implications for Korea	Anne O. Krueger
95-07	Prospects for Northeast Asian Economic Development: Japan's Perspective	Hisao Kanamori

1996

	Title	Author
96-01	Trends of International Financial Market and Prospects of Global Economy in 1996	Allen Sinai
96-02	Future European Model: Economic Internationalization and Cultural Decentralization	Jørgen Ørstrøm Møller
96-03	Evolving Role of the OECD in the Global Economy	Donald Johnston
96-04	The Political Context and Consequences of East Asian Economic Growth	Francis Fukuyama
96-05	Korea's New Global Responsibilities	A. W. Clausen

1997

	Title	Author
97-01	East Asia in Overdrive: Multinationals and East Asian Integration	Wendy Dobson
97-02	American Security Policy in the Asia Pacific - Three Crisis and How We Dealt with Them	William Perry
97-03	Public Sector Reform in New Zealand and its Relevance to Korea	Donald Hunn

1998

	Title	Author
98-01	Global Cooperations and National Government: Why We Need Multilateral Agreement on Investment	Edward Graham
98-02	Korean-American Relations: The Search for Stability at a Time of Change	W. Anthony Lake
98-03	Korea: From Vortex to Hub of Northeast Asia	Donald P. Gregg
98-04	German Unification: Economic Consequences and Policy Lessons	Juergen B. Donges
98-05	Globalization and versus Tribalization: The Dilemma at the End of the 20th Century	Guy Sorman

1999

	Title	Author
99-01	Economic and Political Situation in North Korea and Security in Northeast Asia	Marcus Noland
99-02	The International Financial Market and the US Dollar/Yen Exchange Rate: An Overview and Prospects for the Future	Kenneth S. Courtis

	Title	Author
99-03	Prospects and Policy Recommendations for the Korean Economy and Other Asian Economies	Donald Johnston/ Hubert Neiss
99-04	Reflections on Contrasting Present-day US and Japanese Economic Performances	Hugh Patrick
99-05	Challenge for the World Economy: Where Do the Risks Lie?	Rudiger Dornbusch

2000

	Title	Author
00-01	North Korea-US Relationship: Its Current Condition and Future Prospects	Stephen W. Bosworth
00-02	Global New Economy: Challenges and Opportunities for Korea	Soogil Young
00-03	Global Trend in Financial Supervision	YongKeun Lee
00-04	Asia Grows, Japan Slows: Prospects for the World Economy and Markets	Kenneth S. Courtis
00-05	The Future of International Financial System and its Implications for Korea	Morris Goldstein
00-06	Prospects for Millennium Round Trade Negotiations and Korea-US Free Trade Agreement	Jeffrey Schott/ InBeom Choi
00-07	Prospects for the Multilateral Economic Institutions	Anne O. Krueger
00-08	Avoiding Apocalypse: The Future of the Two Koreas	Marcus Noland
00-09	Attracting FDI in the Knowledge Era	Andrew Fraser
00-10	The Economic and Foreign Policies of the New US Administration and Congress	C. Fred Bergsten
00-11	Korea and the US: Partners in Prosperity and Security	Stephen W. Bosworth
00-12	The Outlook for Asia and Other Emerging Markets in 2000	Charles H. Dallara/ Robert Hormats
00-13	Relationship between Corporation and Finance: Current Status and Prospects	Youngkeun Lee
00-14	How Should Korea Cope with Financial Globalization	James P. Rooney

2001

	Title	Author
01-01	The US Economy on the Brink? Japan on the Edge? Implications for Korea	Kenneth S. Courtis
01-02	The Economic Policy of the Bush Administration toward Korea	Marcus Noland

	Title	Author
01-03	Overcoming 3Cs	Jeffrey D. Jones
01-04	High Tech, The Consequences for our Relationship with Technology on our Lives and Businesses	John Naisbitt
01-05	Korea and the IMF	Stanley Fischer
01-06	The Status of Korea's Restructuring: An Outlook over the Next 10 Years	Dominic Barton
01-07	The World Dollar Standard and the East Asian Exchange Rate Dilemma	Ronald McKinnon
01-08	Europe's Role in Global Governance and Challenges to East Asia	Pierre Jacquet

2002

	Title	Author
02-01	Managing Capital Inflows: The Chilean Experience	Carlos Massad
02-02	Globalization and Korea: Opportunities and Backlash and Challenges	Martin Wolf
02-03	The US-Japan Economic Relationship and Implications for Korea	Marcus Noland
02-04	US Global Recovery: For Real? - Prospects and Risks	Allen Sinai
02-05	Globalization: A Force for Good	Patricia Hewitt
02-06	The World after 9/11: A Clash of Civilization?	Francis Fukuyama
02-07	Hanging Together: On Monetary and Financial Cooperation in Asia	Barry Eichengreen
02-08	The Global Economy Rebounds - But How Fast and For How Long? Issues and Implications for Korea and Asia	Kenneth S. Courtis
02-09	The US Economy and the Future of the Dollar: An Outlook for the World Economy	Marcus Noland
02-10	The Doha Round: Objectives, Problems and Prospects	Jagdish Bhagwati
02-11	The Outlook for Korea and the Global Economy 2002-2003	Paul F. Gruenwald
02-12	The US and World Economy: Current Status and Prospects	John B. Taylor
02-13	9/11 and the US Approach to the Korean Peninsula	Thomas C. Hubbard
02-14	The Outlook for US Economy, the Dollar and US Trade Policy	C. Fred Bergsten
02-15	New Challenges and Opportunities for the Global Telecommunications and Information Industries	Peter F. Cowhey

2003

	Title	Author
03-01	The US and World Economy: After the Iraq War	Allen Sinai
03-02	Korea in the OECD Family	Donald Johnston
03-03	The New Role of the US in the Asia-Pacific	Charles Morrison
03-04	The Global Economic Outlook and the Impact of President Bush's Economic Stimulus Package	Phil Gramm
03-05	Europe and Germany in Transition, Where Will the Economies Go?	Hans Tietmeyer
03-06	Regional Financial Cooperation in East Asia	Eisuke Sakakibara
03-07	The Global Exchange Rate Regime and Implications for East Asian Currencies	John Williamson

2004

	Title	Author
04-01	General Outlook on the US and World Economy in 2004	Allen Sinai
04-02	Korea after Kim Jong-il	Marcus Noland
04-03	US-Japan Relations and Implications for Korea	Hugh Patrick/ Gerald Curtis
04-04	China's Economic Rise and New Regional Growth Paradigm	Zhang Yunling
04-05	The Case for a Common Currency in Asia	Robert Mundell
04-06	A Foreign Businessman's Observations on Korean Economy and Other Things	William C. Oberlin

2005

	Title	Author
05-01	US Trade Policy after the 2004 US Election	Peter F. Cowhey
05-02	Asia in Transition and Implications for Korea	Dominic Barton
05-03	Post-Election US and Global Economies: Market Prospects, Risks, and Issues	Allen Sinai
05-04	The Korean Economy: A Critical Assessment from the Japanese Perspective	Yukiko Fukagawa
05-05	The Blind Man and the Elephant: Competing Perspectives on Global Imbalances	Barry Eichengreen
05-06	Mutual Interdependence: Asia and the World Economy	Anne O. Krueger

		Title	Author
05-07		The Impact of China and India on the Global Economy	Wendy Dobson
05-08		Economic Integration between East Asia and Asia-Pacific	Robert Scollay
05-09		Moody's Perspective on Korea's Ratings	Thomas Byrne

2006

		Title	Author
06-01		Oil Prices, Ben Bernanke, Inflation, and the Fourth Energy Recession	Philip K. Verleger
06-02		US and Global Economy and Financial Market Prospects: Picking up Steam	Allen Sinai
06-03		Korea-US FTA: A Path to Sustainable Growth	Alexander Vershbow
06-04		Japan's Foreign Policy for Economy and Japan-Korea FTA	Oshima Shotaro
06-05		Japan's Economic Recovery: Implications for Korea	Yukiko Fukagawa
06-06		M&A in the 21st Century and its Implications	Robert F. Bruner
06-07		Korea's Growing Stature in the Global Economy	Charles H. Dallara
06-08		Asian Economic Integration and Common Asian Currency	Eisuke Sakakibara
06-09		Measuring American Power in Today's Complex World and China "Rising": What Lessons for Today from the Past?	Paul Kennedy/ Bernard Gordon
06-10		- Whither China? - The Global Scramble for IT Leadership: Winners and Losers	- Richard N. Cooper - George Scalise

2007

		Title	Author
07-01		Korea and the United States - Forging a Partnership for the Future: A View from Washington	Edwin J. Feulner
07-02		Germany: Understanding for the Underperformance since Reunification	Juergen B. Donges
07-03		Seismic Shifts, the World Economy, and Financial Markets in 2007	Allen Sinai
07-04		Changing Economic Environment: Their Implications for Korea	Angel Gurría
07-05		The Feasibility of Establishing an East Asian FTA: A Chinese Perspective	Zhang Yunling
07-06		The Global Oil and Gas Market: Paradigm Shift and Implications for Korea	Fereidun Fesharaki

	Title	Author
07-07	The Changing World Economy and Implications for Korea	Anne O. Krueger
07-08	The Longest Recovery of the Japanese Economy: Prospects and Challenges	Yukiko Fukagawa
07-09	Digital Networked Economy and Global Corporate Strategy	Ben Verwaayen
07-10	Moving Forward on the KORUS FTA: Now for the Hard Time	Jeffrey Schott
07-11	The Korean Economy and the FTA with the United States	Barry Eichengreen
07-12	- The Outlook for East Asian Economic Integration: Coping with American Protectionism, Chinese Power, and Japanese Recovery - Economic Outlook for Korea and the Region	- David Hale - Jerald Schiff
07-13	- Why the US Will Continue to Lead the 21st Century? - The Outlook of the Indian Economy from Business Perspective: Implications for Korean Business	- Guy Sorman - Tarun Das

2008

	Title	Author
08-01	Successes of Globalization: the Case of Korea	Anne O. Krueger
08-02	The US "Risk" to Asia and Global Expansion	Allen Sinai
08-03	Europe's Slow Growth: A Warning for Korea	Guy Sorman
08-04	Global Challenges that Will Confront the Next US President	James A. Baker III
08-05	Current Status and Prospects of the Japanese Capital Markets	Atsushi Saito
08-06	Economic and Political Outlook for America and their Implications to the World	Phil Gramm
08-07	The Outlook of the Regional and Global Economic and Financial Situation: Perspectives on International Banking	Charles H. Dallara
08-08	Can South Korea Still Compete?	Guy Sorman
08-09	- Sovereign Wealth Funds: Perceptions and Realities - Global Financial Markets under Stress	- Robert C. Pozen - Jeffrey R. Shafer

2009

	Title	Author
09-01	Global and Regional Economic Developments and Prospects, and the Implications for Korea	Subir Lall
09-02	Competing in an Era of Turbulence and Transition	Deborah Wince-Smith
09-03	US and Global Economic and Financial Crisis: Prospects, Policies, and Perspectives	Allen Sinai
09-04	US Trade Policy in the Obama Era	Jeffrey Schott
09-05	Beyond Keynesianism	Justin Yifu Lin
09-06	- Current Crisis and the Impact on Developing Countries - Lessons from the Current Economic Crisis	- Danny Leipziger - Anne O. Krueger
09-07	- Obama, Can It Work? - The US-Korea Economic Partnership: Working Together in a Time of Global Crisis	- Guy Sorman - Jeffrey Schott

2010

	Title	Author
10-01	The EU in Transition in the New Global Paradigm: Opportunities for Korea	Jean-Pierre Lehmann
10-02	Aftermath of the 'Crises': US and Global Prospects, Legacies, and Policies	Allen Sinai
10-03	The Global Economy: Where Do We Stand?	Anne O. Krueger
10-04	- Japan and Korea in Globalization and its Backlash: Challenges and Prospects - An Overview of China: Economic Prospects and Challenges	- Yukiko Fukagawa - Danny Leipziger
10-05	- Emerging Markets and New Frontiers - Asia in the Global Economy	- Mark Mobius - Dominique Strauss-Kahn
10-06	Rebalancing the World Economy	Paul A. Volcker

2011

	Title	Author
11-01	After the Crisis: What Next in 2011 and 2012?	Allen Sinai
11-02	Safety and Economics of Nuclear Power	SoonHeung Chang
11-03	A Special Lecture on the Rebalancing of the Chinese Economy	Yu Yongding

	Title	Author
11-04	Reshaping the Global Financial Landscape: An Asian Perspective	Institute for Global Economics
11-05	- Economic Outlook and Future Challenges in Developing Asia - Europe's Financial Woes	- Haruhiko Kuroda - Richard N. Cooper
11-06	- Can the G20 Save Globalization and Multilateralism? - Markets, Economic Changes, and Political Stability in North Korea	- Danny Leipziger - Marcus Noland

2012

	Title	Author
12-01	US and Global Economy and Financial Markets in Turmoil: What Lies Ahead?	Allen Sinai
12-02	- Advancement and Education of Science and Technology University and Economic Growth - Prospects of the Eurozone Crisis and its Implications for the Global Economy	- Nam Pyo Suh - Hans Martens
12-03	- The US Elections in 2012 and the Future of US Asia-Pacific Policy - Current Economic Affairs and the Financial Market - An Optimist View on the Global Economy	- Charles Morrison - Charles H. Dallara - Guy Sorman
12-04	- FTAs, Asia-Pacific Integration and Korea - The Eurozone Crisis: Update and Outlook	- Peter A. Petri - Nicolas Véron
12-05	- China's New Leadership and Economic Policy Challenges - Can the WTO Be Resuscitated? Implications for Korea and the Asia Pacific	- Andrew Sheng - Jean-Pierre Lehmann

2013

	Title	Author
13-01	After the Crisis: What Next in 2011 and 2012?	Allen Sinai
13-02	The Eurozone Crisis and its Impact on the Global Economy	Guntram B. Wolff
13-03	- The European Sovereign Debt Crisis: Challenges and How to Solve Them - The Global Outlook: Grounds for Optimism, but Risks Remain Relevant	- Andreas Dombret - John Lipsky
13-04	- The State and Outlook of the US and Chinese Economy - Japan's Abenomics and Foreign Policy	- David Hale - Hugh Patrick/ Gerald Curtis

	Title	Author
13-05	- The Creative Economy and Culture in Korea - Abenomics, Future of the Japanese Economy and the TPP	- Guy Sorman - Yukiko Fukagawa/ Jeffrey Schott
13-06	- Unified Germany in Europe: An Economic Perspective - Chinese Economic Policymaking: A Foreigners' Perspective	- Karl-Heinz Paqué - Bob Davis
13-07	- The Outlook for Japan under Abenomics and Abenationalism - After the Pax Americana (Korea-China-Japan Political and Economic Relation: Whither to?)	- David Asher - David Filling

2014

	Title	Author
14-01	U.S. and Global Economics-Poised for Better Times	- Allen Sinai
14-02	- Abe in the Driver's Seat: Where is the Road Leading? - The Secret of Germany's Performance: The Mittelstand Economy	- Gerald Curtis - Peter Friedrich
14-03	- The Eurozone Economy: Out of the Doldrums? - The Globla Economy 2014	- Karl-Heinz Paqué - Martin Feldstein
14-04	Philanthropy and Welfare	- Guy Sorman
14-05	- Global Trade Environment and the Future of the World Economy - From BRICs to America	- Roberto Azevêdo - Sung Won Sohn
14-06	- Risks and Opportunities in the Global Economic Recovery - Abe's Labor Reform and Innovative Strategies	- Charles H. Dallara - Yukiko Fukagawa
14-07	- China's Economy and Anti-Corruption Drive - US Fed's QE Ending & Asian Financial Markets - China's New Economic Strategies and the Korea-China FTA	- Bob Davis - Anoop Singh - Zhang Yunling

2015

	Title	Author
15-01	- Will the Global Economy Normalize in 2015?	- Allen Sinai
15-02	- The EU Economy in 2015: Will It Take Off? - U.S.-Korea Economic Relations: Partnership for Shared Economic Prosperity - The Hartz Labor Reforms of Germany and the Implications for Korea	- Jeroen Dijsselbloem - Mark W. Lippert - Peter Hartz
15-03	- What Makes China Grow? - What can Korea Learn from Europe's Slow Growth?	- Lawrence Lau - Guy Sorman

	Title	Author
15-04	- Global Energy and Environmental Issues and Switzerland - The Emerging New Asian Economic Disorder	- H.E. Doris Leuthard - David L. Asher
15-05	- The Chinese Economy: Transition towards the New Normal - Germany's Industry 4.0: Harnessing the Potential of Digitization	- Huang Yiping - Matthias Machnig
15-06	- Four Global Forces Changing the World - Turbulence in Emerging Markets and Impact on Korea	- Dominic Barton - Sung-won Sohn
15-07	- Observations on the Korean Economy and North Korea's Economic Potential - Perspectives on China's Economy and Economic Reform	- Thomas Byrne - Huang Haizhou

2016

	Title	Author
16-01	- The U.S. and Global Prospects and Markets in 2016: A Look Ahead	- Allen Sinai
16-02	- The Key Themes and Risks of the Global Economy in 2016 - The U.S. in the Global Economy	- Hung Tran - Anne Krueger
16-03	- The Prospects and Impact of the U.S. Election and Economy - The US and Northeast Asia in a Turbulent Time	- Martin Feldstein - Gerald Curtis
16-04	- The U.S. Presidential Election and Its Economic and Security Implications - The World Economy at a Time of Monetary Experimentation and Political Fracture - Allies in Business: The Future of the U.S.-ROK Economic Relationship	- Marcus Noland & Sung-won Sohn - Charles H. Dallara - Mark Lippert

2017

	Title	Author
17-01	- Big Changes, Big Effects - U.S. and Global Economic and Financial Prospects 2017	- Allen Sinai
17-02	- The 2017 US and Global Macroeconomic Outlook - Automation, Jobs and the Future of Work in Korea	- Martin Feldstein - Jonathan Woetzel
17-03	- Trump's US, Japan's Economy and Korea - Between Brexit and Trump: Global Challenges for the European Union	- Gerald Curtis & Hugh Paztrick - Thomas Wieser
17-04	- The Future of Work: Is This Time Different?	- Carl Benedikt Frey

	Title	Author
17-05	- The Future of Growth - The Current State of US Economy and Trump Administration's Trade Policy with Special Reference to the KORUS FTA Revision	- Simon Baptist - Sung-won Sohn & Jeffrey Schott

2018

	Title	Author
18-01	- Dr. Martin Feldstein's Analysis of the US and Global Economy - U.S. and Global Prospects Looking Ahead	- Martin Feldstein - Allen Sinai
18-02	- US Protectionism, China's Political Shift and Their Implications - Japan's Labor Reform and Future Korea-Japan Cooperation	- Kenneth Courtis - Yukiko Fukagawa
18-03	- U.S. Economic and Trade Policy for Korea and Asia - How Europeans See China, Changing World Order and Its Implications for Korea	- Charles Freeman - Guy Sorman
18-04	- Asia's New Economic Landscape: India, Japan and China - Climate, Energy and Green Tech: Transforming Our Economies	- Eisuke Sakakibara - Karsten Sach

2019

	Title	Author
19-01	- Financial Innovation, FinTech and the Future of Finance - Setting up Canada's National Pension System for Success – CPPIB's Perspectives	- Robert Merton - Suyi Kim
19-02	- Why I Remain Optimistic about China: Why China's Worst Enemy in the Short-Term Will Prove its Best Friend in the Long-Term - The World in 2019: U.S., Global Economies, Policies and Markets – Can Expansion be sustained?	- Henny Sender - Allen Sinai
19-03	- A Brief Tour of Global Near-term Risks and Long-run Concerns about the International Financial Architecture - 5 Ways the Financial System Will Fail Next Time	-Carmen Reinhart -Michael Barr
19-04	- Beyond 1980's: The New Horizon of Japan-Korea Economic Relations - Reflections on the Japanese Economy and Abenomics	-Yukiko Fukagawa -Hugh Patrick
19-05	- Financial Innovation and Asset Management Strategies in the Age of Hyper-Low Interest Rates	- Robert Merton
19-06	- Artificial Intelligence (AI) and its Impact on the Future of Economy and Society - U.S.-China, Korea-Japan Trade Disputes and the Global Trading System	- Jerome Glenn - Jeffrey Schott

		Title	Author
19-10	Oct 22	Financial Innovation and Asset Management Strategies in the Age of Hyper−Low Interest Rates	Robert Merton
19-11	Nov 19	Artificial Intelligence (AI) and its Impact on the Future of Economy and Society	Jerome Glenn

2020

		Title	Author
20-01	Jan 16	Charting 'Uncharted Waters': The U.S. and World in 2020	Allen Sinai
20-02	May 28	The 30th Anniversary of the German Reunification: Lessons and Policy Implications	Stephan Auer

2021

	Title	Author
21-01	- Geopolitical Challenges and Opportunities in East Asia Under the Biden Administration - Emerging Trends and Issues for International Capital Markets and BlackRock's ESG Strategy - 2021 Global and Asia Pacific Regional Economic Outlook - Prospects for the U.S. and Global Economies and Financial Markets in 2021	- Evans J.R. Revere - Henny Sender - Shaun Roache - Allen Sinai
21-02	- Biden Administration's Foreign Policy on Asia: Prospects for US-China Relations and Implications for Korea - The Future of International Trading System under the Biden Administration and Its Implications for Korea: Whither US Commercial Policy toward Asia?	- Victor Cha - Jeffrey J. Schott

2022

	Title	Author
22-01	- The Future of Cryptocurrency - Perspectives on ESG Investing from CPP Investments & Prospects for International Financial Markets - China's Economy at a Crossroads: Implications for US-China Relations and Korea	- Brian Brooks - Suyi Kim - David Dollar
22-02	- 2022 Prospects for Global Economy and Trade, and Implications for Korea - Geopolitical Risk Proliferation and Role of the ROK-US Alliance: Policy Implications for the New Korean administration - New Challenges for World Trade after Russia's Invasion of Ukraine	- Anne Krueger - Victor Cha - Jeffrey J. Schott

2023

	Title	Author
23-01	- Navigating the Global Multiple Economic Crises: Geopolitical and Policy Implications for Korea - US-Korea Alliance: New Challenges, New Strength - Supply Chain Crisis: Myths and Realities - Global Financial Market Turmoil Emergency Check: Asia, are we going under again?	- Charles H. Dallara - Evans J.R. Revere - Robert Dohner - Tai Hui
23-02	- The Future of US-China Decoupling Amid Weakening Chinese Economic Prospects - S.Korea diplomatic and security policy review and Implications for cooperation with US & Japan - US-China Conflict: A New Roadmap to Restoring Mutually Advantageous Relationship - 2023 Global Economic Prospects and the Challenges for Korea	- Nicholas R. Lardy - Victor Cha - Stephen Roach - Robert Subbaraman

2024

	Title	Author
24-01	- The Bitcoin Spot ETF and Its Implications for the Future of Finance - The Road Ahead: Key Global Geopolitical Challenges and Path Forward to 2024 - 2024 Global Trade and East Asia Economy Outlook: The Future of Korea-Japan Cooperation	- Brian Brooks - Gi-Wook Shin - Fukagawa Yukiko

2025

	Title	Author
25-01	Korea's Political and Security Crisis: U.S.-ROK Alliance and North Korea Strategy under Trump 2.0	Victor Cha

세계경제연구원 간행물

Occasional Paper Series

1993

연 번	제 목	저 자
93-01	Clintonomics and the New World Order: Implications for Korea-US Relations	C. Fred Bergsten
93-02	The Uruguay Round, NAFTA, and US-Korea Economic Relations	Jeffrey Schott

1994

연 번	제 목	저 자
94-01	21세기 준비 어떻게 할 것인가	Paul Kennedy
94-02	미국과 일본 간의 기술경쟁과 한국에 미칠 영향	Ronald A. Morse
94-03	일본경제, 무엇이 문제인가	Toyoo Gyohten
94-04	미국경제와 세계경제: 현황과 전망	Allen Sinai
94-05	국제환율제도 이대로 좋은가	John Williamson
94-06	The Promises of the WTO for the Trading Community	Arthur Dunkel

1995

연 번	제 목	저 자
95-01	멕시코 페소화 위기와 세계금융시장 동향	Charles H. Dallara
95-02	세계경제 동향과 미국경제 전망	Allen Sinai
95-03	새로운 게임, 새로운 규칙과 새로운 전략	Lester Thurow
95-04	미국·북한관계 전망	Robert Scalapino
95-05	미국의 동아시아 정책과 한반도	James A. Baker Ⅲ
95-06	미일 무역마찰과 한국	Anne O. Krueger
95-07	동북아경제권 개발 전망: 일본의 시각	Hisao Kanamori

1996

연 번	제 목	저 자
96-01	Trends of International Financial Market and Prospects of Global Economy in 1996	Allen Sinai
96-02	유럽연합(EU)의 앞날과 세계경제	Jørgen Ørstrøm Møller
96-03	세계경제와 OECD의 역할	Donald Johnston
96-04	동아시아 경제성장의 정치적 배경과 영향	Francis Fukuyama

연 번	제 목	저 자
96-05	국제사회에서의 한국의 새 역할	A. W. Clausen

1997

연 번	제 목	저 자
97-01	다국적기업과 동아시아 경제통합	Wendy Dobson
97-02	아태 지역에 대한 미국의 안보정책	William J. Perry
97-03	뉴질랜드의 공공부문 개혁	Donald Hunn

1998

연 번	제 목	저 자
98-01	범세계적 기업과 다자간 투자협정	Edward M. Graham
98-02	변화 속의 안정: 새로운 한미 관계의 모색	W. Anthony Lake
98-03	한국: 동북아의 새로운 협력 중심으로	Donald P. Gregg
98-04	경제적 측면에서 본 독일 통일의 교훈	Juergen B. Donges
98-05	세계화와 종족화: 20세기 말의 딜레마	Guy Sorman

1999

연 번	제 목	저 자
99-01	북한의 정치·경제 상황과 동북아 안보	Marcus Noland
99-02	엔-달러 환율과 국제금융시장	Kenneth S. Courtis
99-03	한국과 아시아 경제: 전망과 정책대응	Donald Johnston/ Hubert Neiss
99-04	미국과 일본경제의 비교평가	Hugh Patrick
99-05	세계경제: 도전과 전망	Rudiger Dornbusch

2000

연 번	제 목	저 자
00-01	한미관계: 번영과 안보의 동반자	Stephen W. Bosworth
00-02	글로벌 뉴 이코노미: 도전과 한국의 활로	양수길
00-03	금융감독의 세계적 조류	이용근
00-04	성장하는 아시아와 침체 속의 일본	Kenneth S. Courtis
00-05	세계금융체제의 미래와 우리의 대응	Morris Goldstein
00-06	시애틀 이후의 WTO와 한미FTA전망	Jeffrey Schott/ 최인범
00-07	다자간 국제경제기구의 미래와 전망	Anne O. Krueger
00-08	남북한 관계: 현황과 전망	Marcus Noland

연 번	제 목	저 자
00-09	Knowledge 시대의 외국인 직접투자 유치	Andrew Fraser
00-10	미국 新행정부 및 의회의 대외·경제정책방향	C. Fred Bergsten
00-11	한미관계: 번영과 안보의 동반자	Stephen W. Bosworth
00-12	2000년 국제금융 및 신흥시장 전망	Charles H. Dallara/ Robert Hormats
00-13	기업·금융 관계: 현황과 전망	이용근
00-14	금융세계화, 어떻게 대처하나	James P. Rooney

2001

연 번	제 목	저 자
01-01	2001년 미국, 일본경제와 아시아	Kenneth S. Courtis
01-02	부시행정부의 對韓 경제정책과 한국의 대응	Marcus Noland
01-03	3C를 극복하자	Jeffrey D. Jones
01-04	하이테크와 비즈니스, 그리고 세계경제	John Naisbitt
01-05	한국과 IMF	Stanley Fischer
01-06	한국경제의 향후 10년	Dominic Barton
01-07	세계 달러본위제도와 동아시아 환율딜레마	Ronald McKinnon
01-08	新국제질서 속의 유럽과 한국	Pierre Jacquet

2002

연 번	제 목	저 자
02-01	금융위기 再發 어떻게 막나: 칠레의 경험을 중심으로	Carlos Massad
02-02	세계경제의 기회와 위험	Martin Wolf
02-03	美·日 경제현황과 한국의 대응	Marcus Noland
02-04	미국경제와 세계경제: 회복가능성과 위험	Allen Sinai
02-05	세계화: 혜택의 원동력	Patricia Hewitt
02-06	9·11테러사태 이후의 세계질서: 문명의 충돌인가?	Francis Fukuyama
02-07	아시아지역의 통화·금융 협력	Barry Eichengreen
02-08	세계경제, 회복되나?	Kenneth S. Courtis
02-09	미국경제와 달러의 장래	Marcus Noland
02-10	도하라운드: 문제점과 전망	Jagdish Bhagwati
02-11	2003 한국경제와 세계경제 전망	Paul F. Gruenwald
02-12	미국경제 현황과 세계경제의 앞날	John B. Taylor
02-13	9·11사태와 미국의 한반도정책	Thomas C. Hubbard
02-14	미국 경제, 달러 및 대외통상정책 방향	C. Fred Bergsten
02-15	미국의 IT산업 관련 정책과 한국	Peter F. Cowhey

2003

연 번	제 목	저 자
03-01	이라크전 이후의 미국경제와 세계경제	Allen Sinai
03-02	OECD가 본 한국경제	Donald Johnston
03-03	아태 지역에서의 미국의 새 역할	Charles Morrison
03-04	세계경제 전망과 부시행정부의 경기부양책	Phil Gramm
03-05	침체된 독일·유럽 경제가 주는 정책적 교훈과 시사	Hans Tietmeyer
03-06	동아시아 금융협력과 한국	Eisuke Sakakibara
03-07	세계환율체제 개편과 동아시아 경제	John Williamson

2004

연 번	제 목	저 자
04-01	2004 미국경제와 세계경제 전망	Allen Sinai
04-02	김정일 이후의 한반도	Marcus Noland
04-03	미국 대통령 선거와 韓·美·日관계	Hugh Patrick/ Gerald Curtis
04-04	중국경제의 부상과 동북아 지역경제	Zhang Yunling
04-05	아시아 화폐단일화, 가능한가?	Robert Mundell
04-06	외국기업인의 눈에 비친 한국경제	William C. Oberlin

2005

연 번	제 목	저 자
05-01	대통령선거 이후의 미국 통상정책, 어떻게 되나	Peter F. Cowhey
05-02	아시아 경제·무역환경, 어떻게 전개되나?	Dominic Barton
05-03	제2기 부시 행정부의 경제정책과 세계경제 및 시장 전망	Allen Sinai
05-04	일본의 시각에서 본 한국경제의 활로	Yukiko Fukagawa
05-05	세계경제, 무엇이 문제인가	Barry Eichengreen
05-06	세계 속의 한국경제: 역할과 전망	Anne O. Krueger
05-07	중국과 인도가 세계경제에 미치는 영향	Wendy Dobson
05-08	동아시아와 아태지역 경제통합	Robert Scollay
05-09	국제신용평가기관이 보는 한국	Thomas Byrne

2006

연 번	제 목	저 자
06-01	고유가와 세계경제의 앞날	Philip K. Verleger
06-02	2006년 미국경제/세계경제와 금융시장 전망	Allen Sinai

연 번	제 목	저 자
06-03	한미FTA: 지속성장의 활로	Alexander Vershbow
06-04	일본의 대외경제정책과 한일 FTA	Oshima Shotaro
06-05	일본경제 회생과 한국경제	Yukiko Fukagawa
06-06	세계 M&A시장 현황과 전망: 우리의 대응	Robert F. Bruner
06-07	세계인이 보는 한국경제는?	Charles H. Dallara
06-08	아시아 공통통화와 아시아 경제통합	Eisuke Sakakibara
06-09	미국의 힘은 얼마나 강하며, 중국의 부상은 어떻게 보아야 하는가?	Paul Kennedy/ Bernard Gordon
06-10	- 20년 후의 중국, 어떤 모습일까? - 세계 IT 리더십 경쟁: 승자와 패자	- Richard N. Cooper - George Scalise

2007

연 번	제 목	저 자
07-01	한미관계: 새로운 동반자 시대를 지향하며	Edwin J. Feulner
07-02	통일 이후 독일: 경제침체의 교훈	Juergen B. Donges
07-03	2007년 세계경제와 금융시장의 지각변동	Allen Sinai
07-04	급변하는 세계경제환경, 어떻게 대처해야 하나	Angel Gurría
07-05	동아시아 FTA 가능한가?: 중국의 시각	Zhang Yunling
07-06	구조적 변화 맞고 있는 세계석유시장과 한국	Fereidun Fesharaki
07-07	변모하는 세계경제와 한국	Anne O. Krueger
07-08	되살아나는 일본경제: 전망과 과제	Yukiko Fukagawa
07-09	디지털 네트워크 경제와 글로벌 기업 전략	Ben Verwaayen
07-10	한미FTA: 미국의 시각	Jeffrey Schott
07-11	한미FTA와 한국경제의 미래	Barry Eichengreen
07-12	- 동아시아 경제통합, 어떻게 보나 - 한국경제 및 동아시아경제 전망	- David Hale - Jerald Schiff
07-13	- 21세기는 여전히 미국의 세기가 될 것인가? - 인도경제 전망과 한국 기업	- Guy Sorman - Tarun Das

2008

연 번	제 목	저 자
08-01	국가 미래를 위한 한국의 세계화 전략	Anne O. Krueger
08-02	2008년 미국경제와 세계금융시장 동향	Allen Sinai
08-03	유럽의 경제침체: 우리에게 주는 시사점	Guy Sorman
08-04	차기 미국 대통령이 풀어야할 세계적 도전	James A. Baker III
08-05	일본 자본시장의 현재와 전망	Atsushi Saito

연 번	제 목	저 자
08-06	대선 이후 미국의 정치 · 경제, 어떻게 전개되나?	Phil Gramm
08-07	세계 및 아시아 경제 · 금융 전망	Charles H. Dallara
08-08	한국경제의 경쟁력 강화, 어떻게 하나?	Guy Sorman
08-09	- 국부펀드: 인식과 현실 - 긴장 속의 세계금융시장, 어떻게 되나?	- Robert C. Pozen - Jeffrey R. Shafer

2009

연 번	제 목	저 자
09-01	2009년 한국경제와 세계 및 아시아 경제 전망	Subir Lall
09-02	혼란과 전환기의 경쟁력 강화: 과제와 전망	Deborah Wince-Smith
09-03	위기 속의 미국 및 세계 경제와 금융: 전망과 정책대응	Allen Sinai
09-04	미국 오바마 행정부의 통상정책	Jeffrey Schott
09-05	하강하는 세계경제와 케인지언 정책 처방의 실효성	Justin Yifu Lin
09-06	- 세계금융위기가 개도국에 미치는 여파와 대응 - 최근 세계경제위기의 교훈과 전망	- Danny Leipziger - Anne O. Krueger
09-07	- 미국 오바마 행정부의 경제 및 대외정책, 어떻게 되나? - 한미 경제 파트너십: 세계적 위기에 어떻게 협력할 것인가	- Guy Sorman - Jeffrey Schott

2010

연 번	제 목	저 자
10-01	새로운 세계질서 속에 변화하는 EU: 한국의 기회는?	Jean-Pierre Lehmann
10-02	위기 이후 미국 및 세계경제 전망, 그리고 유산과 정책 과제	Allen Sinai
10-03	세계경제, 어떻게 볼 것인가?: 진단과 전망	Anne O. Krueger
10-04	- 세계화 파고 속의 한국과 일본경제: 도전과 전망 - 중국 경제의 虛와 實	- Yukiko Fukagawa - Danny Leipziger
10-05	- 신흥국 자본시장과 뉴 프런티어 - 세계경제와 아시아의 역할	- Mark Mobius - Dominique Strauss-Kahn
10-06	세계경제의 재균형	Paul A. Volcker

2011

연 번	제 목	저 자
11-01	위기 이후의 세계경제와 한국경제: 2011년 및 2012년 전망	Allen Sinai
11-02	원자력 발전의 안전성과 경제성: 한국의 선택은?	장순흥
11-03	중국 경제의 재(再)균형	Yu Yongding
11-04	세계금융질서의 개편: 아시아의 시각	세계경제연구원
11-05	- 아시아 경제의 발전전망과 도전과제 - 유럽의 국가채무위기: 평가와 전망	- Haruhiko Kuroda - Richard N. Cooper
11-06	- 기로에 선 세계화와 다자주의, 그리고 G-20 - 북한의 시장과 경제, 그리고 정치적 안정성, 어떻게 변화하고 있나?	- Danny Leipziger - Marcus Noland

2012

연 번	제 목	저 자
12-01	혼돈 속의 세계경제와 금융시장: 분석과 2012년 전망	Allen Sinai
12-02	- 카이스트의 혁신 - 유로위기 해결책은 없나	- 서남표 - Hans Martens
12-03	- 2012년 미국의 대선과 향후 아태정책 전망 - 세계경제 및 금융시장 현황 - 그래도 세계경제의 미래는 밝다	- Charles Morrison - Charles H. Dallara - Guy Sorman
12-04	- FTA와 아태지역 통합 그리고 한국 - 유로위기 언제 끝나?	- Peter A. Petri - Nicolas Véron
12-05	- 중국의 새 리더십과 경제정책 - 국제통상질서의 현황과 WTO의 미래	- Andrew Sheng - Jean-Pierre Lehmann

2013

연 번	제 목	저 자
13-01	2013년 세계경제와 미국경제 전망	Allen Sinai
13-02	유로존, 올해는 위기에서 벗어날 수 있나?	Guntram B. Wolff
13-03	- 유럽국채위기: 과제와 해결책 - 세계경제, 언제 회복되나?	- Andreas Dombret - John Lipsky
13-04	- 미국과 중국경제 현황과 전망 - 일본의 아베노믹스와 외교정책	- David Hale - Hugh Patrick/Gerald Curtis
13-05	- 한국의 창조경제와 문화 - 아베노믹스와 일본 경제의 미래, 그리고 TPP	- Guy Sorman - Yukiko Fukagawa/ Jeffrey Schott
13-06	- 통일 독일의 경제·정치적 위상: 한국에 대한 시사점 - 외국인이 바라본 중국의 경제정책	- Karl-Heinz Paqué - Bob Davis

2014

연 번	제 목	저 자
14-01	2014년 세계경제, 나아질 것인가?	Allen Sinai
14-02	- 아베정권은 어디로 가고 있나? - 중견기업: 순항하는 독일경제의 비결	- Gerald Curtis - Peter Friedrich
14-03	- 유럽경제, 살아날 것인가? - 2014년 세계 경제의 향방은?	- Karl-Heinz Paqué - Martin Feldstein
14-04	복지향상과 기부문화	Guy Sorman
14-05	- 세계무역 환경과 세계경제의 미래 - 브릭스(BRICs)에서 미국으로	- Roberto Azevêdo - Sung Won Sohn
14-06	- 세계경제 회복, 위기인가 기회인가 - 아베 정권의 노동개혁과 혁신전략은 성공할 것인가	- Charles H. Dallara - Yukiko Fukagawa
14-07	- 중국경제 현황과 시진핑의 반부패운동 - 다가올 미 연준의 QE종료가 아시아 금융시장에 미칠 영향 - 중국의 신경제 전략과 한-중 FTA	- Bob Davis - Anoop Singh - Zhang Yunling

2015

연 번	제 목	저 자
15-01	2015년 세계경제, 정상화될 것인가	Allen Sinai
15-02	- 2015년 유럽경제, 회복될 것인가? - 공동 번영을 위한 한미 경제 파트너십 - 독일 하르츠 노동개혁과 한국에 대한 시사점	- Jeroen Dijsselbloem - Mark W. Lippert - Peter Hartz
15-03	- 중국 경제의 앞날을 내다보며 - 유럽의 저성장에서 우리는 무엇을 배워야 하는가?	- Lawrence Lau - Guy Sorman
15-04	- 글로벌 에너지(중점)환경 이슈와 스위스의 경험 - 혼돈의 아시아 경제, 어디로 가는가	- H.E. Doris Leuthard - David L. Asher
15-05	- 중국 경제의 신창타이(新常態)는 무엇인가 - 디지털화를 활용한 독일의 산업혁명 4.0	- Huang Yiping - Matthias Machnig
15-06	- 세상을 바꾸는 네 가지 글로벌 흐름 - 격변하는 신흥시장과 한국에 미칠 영향	- Dominic Barton - Sung-won Sohn
15-07	- 내가 본 한국, 한국 경제, 그리고 북한 경제의 잠재력 - 중국의 경제개혁과 향후 전망	- Thomas Byrne - Huang Haizhou

2016

연 번	제 목	저 자
16-01	2016년 세계경제 및 금융시장 전망	- Allen Sinai
16-02	- 2016년 세계 경제의 주요 이슈와 리스크 - 미국의 경제·정치 상황이 세계 경제에 미치는 영향	- Hung Tran - Anne Krueger
16-03	- 미국 경제와 대선이 세계 경제에 미칠 영향 - 미국 대통령 선거가 동북아에 미칠 지정학적 영향과 전망	- Martin Feldstein - Gerald Curtis

연 번	제 목	저 자
16-04	- 미국 새 행정부의 경제와 안보 정책 - 통화정책 실험과 정치 분열기의 세계 경제 - 한미 경제 협력: 현황과 전망	- Marcus Noland & Sung-won Sohn - Charles H. Dallara - Mark Lippert

2017

연 번	제 목	저 자
17-01	- 대변혁 속의 2017 – 미국과 세계 경제 금융 전망	- Allen Sinai
17-02	- 미국 신정부의 경제정책과 2017년 미국 및 세계 경제 전망 - 4차 산업혁명 시대 자동화, 일자리, 그리고 직업의 미래	- Martin Feldstein - Jonathan Woetzel
17-03	- 트럼프의 미국, 일본 경제 그리고 한국 - 브렉시트와 미국의 트럼프 대통령: 유럽의 도전	- Gerald Curtis & Hugh Patrick - Thomas Wieser
17-04	- 직업의 미래 – 이번엔 다른가	- Carl Benedikt Frey
17-05	- 세계경제 성장 전망과 기술의 역할 - 미국경제 현황과 트럼프 행정부의 통상정책 및 한미 FTA 개정	- Simon Baptist - Sung-won Sohn &Jeffrey Schott

2018

연 번	제 목	저 자
18-01	- 펠드스타인 교수가 진단하는 미국과 세계경제 - 2018년 미국과 세계 경제·금융 전망	- Martin Feldstein - Allen Sinai
18-02	- 미국 보호주의와 중국 정치체제 변화의 함의 - 일본 노동개혁과 한일 협력의 미래	- Kenneth Courtis - Yukiko Fukagawa
18-03	- 트럼프 행정부의 한국 및 대아시아 무역·경제 정책 - 유럽이 보는 시진핑 체제하의 중국과 세계 질서	- Charles Freeman - Guy Sorman
18-04	- 새로운 아시아 경제 지평: 일본, 중국 그리고 인도 - 독일의 기후변화, 에너지 및 녹색기술 정책 경험과 한국에 대한 시사점	- Eisuke Sakakibara - Karsten Sach

2019

연 번	제 목	저 자
19-01	- 금융혁신, 핀테크 그리고 금융의 미래 - 캐나다 국민연금 시스템의 성공과 CPPIB	- Robert Merton - Suyi Kim
19-02	- 내가 중국 경제를 여전히 낙관하는 이유: 왜 중국의 단기적 악재가 장기적 호재일까 - 2019년 세계 경제 및 금융 전망 – 과연 경기 확장세는 지속될 것인가?	- Henny Sender - Allen Sinai

연 번	제 목	저 자
19-03	국제금융체제의 단기 리스크와 구조적 문제 향후 금융시스템 실패의 5가지 시나리오	-Carmen Reinhart -Michael Barr
19-04	한·일 무역갈등을 넘어서: 양국 경제관계의 새로운 지평 휴 패트릭 교수가 본 일본경제와 아베노믹스	-Yukiko Fukagawa -Hugh Patrick
19-05	초저금리 시대의 금융 혁신과 자산운용 전략	-Robert Merton
19-06	인공지능(AI)이 만드는 경제·사회의 미래 미·중, 한·일 무역분쟁과 세계무역체제	- Jerome Glenn - Jeffrey Schott

2020

연 번	제 목	저 자
20-01	2020년 미국 및 세계 경제 전망: '미지의 바다' 항해도 그리기 −10개의 메시지와 코로나바이러스 충격	- Allen Sinai
20-02	독일 통일 30년의 경험: 교훈과 정책적 시사점	- Stephan Auer

2021

연 번	제 목	저 자
21-01	− 美 바이든 행정부 출범과 동아시아의 지정학적 도전 및 기회 − 국제금융시장 현황 및 핵심 이슈와 블랙록 ESG투자 전략 − 2021 글로벌 경제 전망: 중국·일본·한국, 아시아 경제의 향방 − 2021년 미국 및 세계 경제 예측과 금융시장 전망	- Evans J.R. Revere - Henny Sender - Shaun Roache - Allen Sinai
21-02	− 바이든 행정부의 아시아 외교정책: 미·중 관계 전망과 한국에 대한 시사점 − 바이든 행정부 출범과 국제통상체제의 미래: 미국의 對아시아 통상전략 향방 및 한국에의 시사점	- Victor Cha - Jeffrey J. Schott

2022

연 번	제 목	저 자
22-01	− 가상화폐의 미래 − 캐나다 연기금(CPP)의 ESG 투자 전략과 국제금융시장 전망 − 전환점에 선 중국 경제: 美 中 역학관계와 한국에의 시사점	- Brian Brooks - Suyi Kim - David Dollar
22-02	− 2022년 글로벌 경제 및 무역 전망: 한국에의 정책적 시사점 − 지정학적 리스크 확산과 한미동맹의 역할: 新 정부 외교 안보 전략 시사점 − 러시아의 우크라이나 침공 이후 세계 무역의 새로운 도전	- Anne Krueger - Victor Cha - Jeffrey J. Schott

2023

연 번	제 목	저 자
23-01	− 글로벌 복합 경제 위기 진단: 한국 경제에의 지정학적 및 정책적 시사점 − 한미동맹의 미래: 새로운 도전, 새로운 기회 − 글로벌 공급망 이슈 진단과 세계 경제안보 전망 − 국제 금융시장 긴급진단 웨비나: 달러 초강세 속 亞 외환위기 재발 위험 진단	- Charles H. Dallara - Evans J.R. Revere - Robert Dohner - Tai Hui
23-02	− 중국경제 둔화 전망과 미중 디커플링의 전략적 함의 − 尹정부 1년 외교안보정책 리뷰 및 한미일 공조를 위한 제언 − 美中 패권 갈등: 互惠 관계 회복을 위한 새로운 로드맵 − 2023년 세계경제 전망과 한국경제의 도전	- Nicholas R. Lardy - Victor Cha - Stephen Roach - Robert Subbaraman

2024

연 번	제 목	저 자
24-01	− 비트코인 현물 ETF 등장: 금융투자 게임체인저 되나 − 글로벌 지정학 위기 진단과 2024년 전망 및 시사점 − 2024년 글로벌 무역과 동아시아 경제 전망: 한일 협력의 미래	- Brian Brooks - Gi-Wook Shin - Fukagawa Yukiko

2025

연 번	제 목	저 자
25-01	한국 정치·안보 위기 긴급 진단: 트럼프 2.0 한미동맹의 미래와 대북전략 변화	Victor Cha